About the author:

Robert Chilimidos is a veteran police officer of almost twenty years service. He has served on both local and state police organizations. He has been a member of the California Highway Patrol for fifteen years, over ten of which he has spent as an auto theft investigator. He has attended the University of California at Berkeley, and Sacramento State and City Colleges. He has been instructor in auto theft investigation at the California Highway Patrol Academy, and is presently an instructor in the Police Science Department at Sacramento City College. He is a member and past president of Lambda Epsilon Police Fraternity, and a member of the International Association of Auto Theft Investigators. He is well known to law enforcement agencies in California but his knowledge of auto theft crime is not limited to the local scene since he has had wide experience on the national and international scene as well. He has frequently testified both in local and federal courts as an expert witness in the field of auto theft.

II

AUTO
THEFT
INVESTIGATION

ROBERT S. CHILIMIDOS

LEGAL BOOK CORP.
316 W. Second St.
Los Angeles, Calif.

Standard Book Number 910874-18-2

Library of Congress Card Number 79-155290

Printed in the United States of America

IV

ERATTA

Page 45 — 15th line should read:
Missing at 8 A.M. on 1-25-70

Page 77 — 8th line should read:
Earle, Earl

Page 111 — Title under Illus. 31 should read:
Engine number prior to 1954

— Title under Illus. 32 should read:
Vehicle identification number affixed to door post

Page 127 — Illus. 45 and 46 are reversed

Page 133 — Illus.48 title should read:
Location of Vehicle identification numbers on Ford Motor
Co. vehicles.

Page 142 — Illus. 50 should read:
1965-1967 Corvette vehicle identification number riveted to
body brace under dashboard.
63-64 spot welded
65-67 riveted

Page 182 — After third line — next six lines should read:
1 Valient   6 cyl.
3 Belvedere   6 cyl.
5 Fury   6 cyl.
P Fury   V8
R Belvedere   V8
V Valiant   V8

Page 187 — Under Pontiac 844 V 1234
First number designates engine number
Second number designates series model

Page 197 — Illus. 59 and 60 are reversed

Page 212 — Truck vehicle identification number locations should be on
page 213

Page 213 — Trailer vehicle identification number locations should be on
page 212

MY THANKS TO ROB, MIKE AND STEVE

MY THANKS ALSO
TO CLAIRE STEWART AND BETTY PERKINS

ACKNOWLEGEMENTS

My sincere thanks to the Director of the Federal Bureau of Investigation, Mr. J. Edgar Hoover, and to the California Highway Patrol, California Department of Motor Vehicles, Oregon State Police, Sacramento Police Department, Minneapolis Police Department, Ontario (Canada) Provincial Police and the National Auto Theft Bureau for providing me with and allowing me to use their forms and graphs.

CONTENTS

AUTO
THEFT
INVESTIGATION

. . . from the beginning

INTRODUCTION

This book was not prepared with the intent that all police officers should or will be auto theft specialists. Rather, it was prepared to familiarize the officer on patrol in the field with some of the problems presented by the crime of auto theft, some hints of what clues to look for, and the laws applicable to the theft of motor vehicles.

Vehicle thefts are rising at an alarming rate and each year a substantial increase in this crime is experienced. Certainly all crimes present a problem to the police, some crimes, however, much more than others and the fact that vehicles are reported stolen at the rate of about one each minute indicates that auto theft is one of the larger problems facing law enforcement today. Vehicle theft today is a big business and it has all the prospects of being even a larger business tomorrow. The auto thief is quite often responsible for other crimes too. In many cases the stolen vehicle may be an untraceable means of transportation for the commission of any number of the other

crimes. Many persons have started stealing cars, then gradu-
ated into other crimes. The motor vehicle affords the criminal
the means with which to evade arrest. Within a matter of a
few hours he can be out of town, into another state, across
the country, or into another country. Because the criminal has
little regard for city limits, county lines or state borders, the
auto theft problem must not be considered only as a local problem. Almost half of the stolen cars are recovered in jurisdictions
other than the one reporting the theft.

Auto theft IS a major crime and as such should not be
given secondary consideration by law enforcement officers,
the public or the courts. Daily we read articles in newspapers
about police officers arresting persons involved in crimes such
as burglary or the passing of worthless checks. More often than
not these articles and pictures of the recovered loot or the
persons arrested are printed on the front page. But when auto
thieves are apprehended, even when the crime involves many
vehicles or vehicles completely stripped, the article is brief
and usually buried on a back page, if such article is printed
at all. The auto theft problem must be brought to everybody's
attention and everybody must make a concentrated effort towards suppressing this crime.

Dedicated people have been combating disease since the
beginning of time, and as a result many thousands of books
have been written about medicine. As many, or more, books
have been written about history. We know, from reading the
Bible, that crime and law enforcement date back to the beginning of time also. However, until a very short time ago, few
books were written concerning crime detection, criminal investigation and the apprehension of criminals as an aid to the
training of law enforcement officers. During earlier years, officers had to learn through the use of the "trial and error"
method or what he could learn from another officer with more
time on the department. This is definitely an out-moded system

and it's practice can not be tolerated in today's application of law enforcement.

The law enforcement officer of today must be a highly trained individual. He must always be on the alert and he cannot take anything for granted. No crime, regardless of it's nature or severity, should go unnoticed. He will match wits with criminals who have had years of experience committing crimes and who have become specialists in certain crimes. They have familiarized themselves with the laws relating to the offense, in an effort to "beat" prosecution, and have equipped themselves with the means by which they may avoid detection and apprehension. The officer must be familiar with current court decisions regarding the constitutional rights of the people, including the criminal, and with the provisions and limitations respecting the search for and seizure of evidence. He must be able to recognize a crime and take the necessary action to apprehend the criminal or to prevent it's repetition. The crime of auto theft must not be an exception.

It is sincerely hoped the material contained in this book will help the police officer (a) develop the ability to make proper appraisals of persons making stolen vehicle reports and the authenticity thereof (b) develop a keen knowledge of what to look for; the vehicle, it's driver, and it's occupants that would be a clue as to whether the vehicle is stolen; (c) develop an understanding of the anti-theft laws peretaining to motor vehicle thefts and embezzlements; (d) to make arrests and recoveries with maximum safety; (e) develop skills in recovering and identifying stolen vehicles, stripped vehicles and components from stripped vehicles, and any evidence from these.

Robert S. Chilimidos
Sacramento, California

1

A SURVEY OF THE STOLEN VEHICLE PROBLEM

The Scope and Cost of the Problem.

With out a doubt, vehicle thefts are one of the costliest crimes, if not the costliest, from which the public suffers. The average loss per each stolen vehicle is approximately 991 dollars, based on all stolen vehicles in the United States.[1] In addition there is, the hard to estimate cost, of countless man hours spent by law enforcement officers in conducting investigations, preparing reports, recovering stolen property, apprehending the thieves and prosecuting them in court, which must be considered in ascertaining the cost of this crime to society. Then added to that, is the dilemma of the vehicle owner who is compelled to pay sky rocketing insurance premiums because of the astronomical increase in insurance claims.

In an effort to develop an understanding of the vehicle theft problem, let us delve into the past for a look at some statistics which graphically illustrate the alarming rise in auto thefts and the consequent economic loss.

1—Figure courtesy Federal Bureau of Investigation, Washington, D.C.

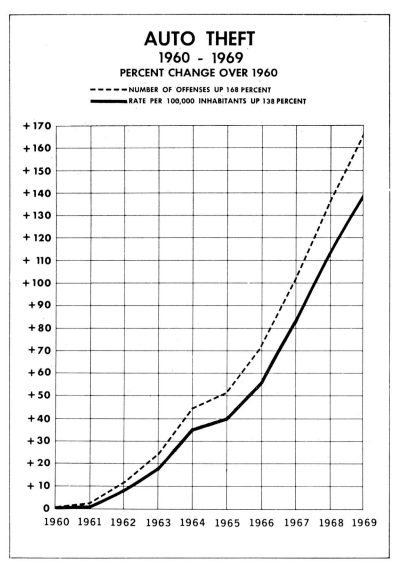

Illus. 1
Courtesy; Federal Bureau of Investigation.

Vehicle Thefts, Recoveries and Number of Vehicles Registered in California.

Year	Stolen[2]	Recovered[3]	Registered[4]
1948	16,246	Not available	4,175,867
1951	17,199	Not available	5,303,524
1956	38,530	35,084	7,065,699
1957	45,178	41,211	7,402,504
1958	46,232	44,769	7,693,590
1959	43,830	42,295	8,086,571
1960	51,189	47,215	8,569,295
1961	51,986	48,578	8,889,860
1962	57,359	53,016	9,647,505
1963	63,717	57,699	9,869,009
1964	75,793	67,947	10,575,237
1965	81,541	69,985	11,191,199
1966	86,929	73,890	11,518,765
1967	97,087	84,495	12,052,030
1968	118,236	97,426	12,495,518
1969	130,693	103,406	13,138,794

Illustration number 1. illustrates the alarming rise in vehicle thefts from 1960 to 1969.

2, 3—California Highway Patrol statistics.
4—California Department of Motor Vehicle statistics.

Vehicle Thefts and Recoveries in the United States[5]

Year	Stolen	Recovered
1956	263,700	246,050
1957	276,000	256,956
1958	282,800	260,176
1959	288,300	265,236
1960	321,400	295,688
1961	326,200	296,842
1962	356,100	320,490
1963	399,000	366,090
1964	463,000	412,070
1965	486,600	428,208
1966	557,000	459,360
1967	654,900	550,814
1968	777,800	668,908
1969	871,900	732,396

During a ten year period from 1953 to 1962, vehicle thefts increased approximately four times faster than the population growth while vehicle registration increased forty-two percent. Thus the rate for this crime increased sixty-three per cent. The rate of increase from 1960 to 1969 was one hundrd sixty-nine percent.[6] The rate of recovery is about ninety percent. Although this recovery rate is an impressive statistic, it does not paint a true picture of the loss suffered by the victims. A vehicle may be reported cleared as recovered but the recovered vehicle may vary from being a complete vehicle to a stripped body only. Some vehicles are recovered with only a fifteen dollar battery missing while others are missing the entire engine, transmission and other components with a replacement value of well over a thousand dollars.

5—Uniform Crime Reports, Federal Bureau of Criminal Investigation.

Persons Arrested For Vehicle Thefts.

Federal Bureau of Investigation figures further reveal that of the persons arrested for vehicle thefts, approximately eighty-seven percent are under the age of twenty-five, and almost sixty-two percent are under the age of eighteen. Many of these youngsters are under the age of sixteen; not even old enough to obtain a drivers license. About forty-one percent of the persons arrested for the first time are involved in the crime of theft of an automobile.

Comparison With Other Crimes.

In order for us to obtain a clear perspective of the vehicle theft picture, let us take a look at some of the other major crimes.

ESTIMATED CRIME INDEX[6]

Year	Murder	Forcible Rape	Robbery	Aggra- vated Assault	Burglary	Larceny ($50 and over)	Auto Theft	(Auto Theft) % of Recovery
1963	8,500	16,400	100,160	147,800	975,900	611,400	399,000	91
1964	9,250	20,550	111,750	184,900	1,110,500	704,500	463,000	89
1965	9,850	22,470	118,920	206,700	1,173,200	762,400	486,600	88
1966	10,920	25,330	153,420	231,800	1,370,300	894,600	557,000	90
1967	12,090	27,100	202,050	253,300	1,605,700	1,047,100	654,900	86
1968	13,650	31,060	261,730	282,400	1,828,900	1,271,100	777,800	86
1969	14,590	36,470	297,580	306,420	1,949,800	1,512,900	871,900	84

6—Uniform Crime Reports, Federal Bureau of Investigation.

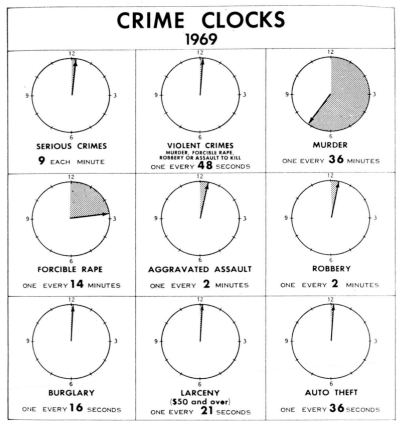

CRIME CLOCKS
1969

SERIOUS CRIMES	**VIOLENT CRIMES**	**MURDER**
9 EACH MINUTE	MURDER, FORCIBLE RAPE, ROBBERY OR ASSAULT TO KILL ONE EVERY **48** SECONDS	ONE EVERY **36** MINUTES
FORCIBLE RAPE	**AGGRAVATED ASSAULT**	**ROBBERY**
ONE EVERY **14** MINUTES	ONE EVERY **2** MINUTES	ONE EVERY **2** MINUTES
BURGLARY	**LARCENY** ($50 and over)	**AUTO THEFT**
ONE EVERY **16** SECONDS	ONE EVERY **21** SECONDS	ONE EVERY **36** SECONDS

Illus. 2.
Courtesy; Federal Bureau of Investigation.

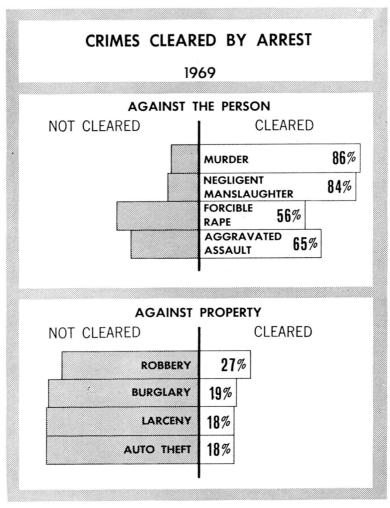

Illus. 3.
Courtesy; Federal Bureau of Investigation.

Illustration number 2 depicts the frequency with which the crimes listed occur, while illustration number 3 gives us an idea as to how many crimes are cleared by arrest. They all tell their story well.

2

LAWS APPLICABLE TO STOLEN
VEHICLE CRIMES

Federal Statutes.

(Title 18, Section 2312 United States Code (Dyer Act). This statute states: "Transportation of stolen vehicle. Whoever transports in interstate or foreign commerce a motor vehicle or aircraft, knowing the same to have been stolen . . .". The meaning of the word "stolen", as used in common law larceny also includes embezzlement or other felonious taking with intent to deprive the owner of his vehicle.

The elements necessary to prove this offense are:
1. The vehicle was reported stolen.
2. The vehicle was transported from one state to another.
3. Suspect had knowledge the vehicle was stolen at the time it was being transported interstate.

Title 18, Section 2313 United States Code. This statute states: "Sale or receipt of stolen vehicle. Whoever receives, conceals, stores, barters, sells, or disposes of any motor vehicle or aircraft moving as, or which is a part of, or which constitutes interstate or foreign commerce, knowing the same to have been stolen . . ."

The elements necessary to prove this offense are:

1. Suspect knew vehicle was stolen.

2. Vehicle was stolen.

3. Suspect concealed vehicle to deprive it's owner of possession or use of the vehicle.

4. Vehicle was moving in interstate or foreign commerce.

California Statutes.

The following California statutes could be used in connection with the various vehicle theft offenses. Statutes of other states can be substituted where applicable.

Penal Code Sections

Penal Code Section 31. Principals to a Crime. (Felony or misdemeanor)

Persons concerned in the commission of a crime; whether they aid, abet, advise, encourage, use force, coercion, threats, or by the use of fraud, compel another to commit any crime.

Penal Code Section 32. Accessories to Crime. (Felony)

Persons who, after a felony has been committed, aids, harbors, or conceals a principal.

Penal Code Section 148. Resisting an Officer in the Discharge of His Duties. (Misdemeanor)

Persons who willfully resist, delay or obstruct an officer from carrying out the duties of his office.

Penal Code Section 148.5. False Reporting of a Crime. (Misdemeanor)

Every person reporting a crime to a peace officer, knowing the report is false.

Penal Code Section 449a. Arson of a Vehicle. (Felony)

Willful and malicious burning of a motor vehicle.

Penal Code Section 450a. Burning with Intent to Defraud Insurer. (Felony)

Burning a vehicle with intentions of collecting money from an insurance company.

Penal Code Section 470. Forgery. (Felony)

Forging the name of an owner of a vehicle upon an ownership certificate with intent to defraud.

Penal Code Section 476a. Issuing a Bad Check. (Felony)

A person who willfully, with intent to defraud, prepares and delivers a check knowing the check to be worthless.

Penal Code Section 484f. Credit Cards, Misuse of. (Felony)

Unauthorized use of a credit card to obtain a vehicle. (Usually involves car rental transactions)

Penal Code Section 487.3. Grand Theft Auto. (Felony)

The taking of another person's vehicle without consent of the owner.

Penal Code Section 484. Theft Defined.

Theft is defined in part; "Every person who shall feloniously steal, take, . . ., or drive away the personal property of another, or who shall fraudulently appropriate property which has been entrusted to him, . . ., is guilty of theft. (The above excerpt is contained in section 484 which defines theft). This section also defines other means by which theft can be accomplished; ". . . knowingly and designedly, by any false or fradu-

lent representation or pretense, defraud any person of
. . . personal property, or who causes or procures
others to report falsely of his wealth or mercantile
character and by thus imposing upon any person, obtains credit and thereby fraudulently . . . obtains
possession . . . of property . . . of another, is guilty of
theft." This section should be referred to when section 484f, 487.3, 503, and 532a are involved.

Penal Code Section 496.1. Receiving Stolen Property. (Felony)
Buying, receiving, concealing or possession of stolen
property knowing the property to be stolen.

**Penal Code Section 497. Bringing Stolen Property
Into State (California).** (Felony or Misdemeanor depending on class of crime in the other state)
Bringing into California stolen or embezzled property from another state or country.

**Penal Code Section 499b. Taking Motor Vehicle for
Temporary Use.** (Misdemeanor)
The taking of a vehicle without the owner's permission and temporarily using it. This is known as
the "joy riding" section.

Penal Code Section 503. Embezzlement defined.
Embezzlement is the fraudulent appropriation of
property by a person to whom it has been entrusted.

**Penal Code Section 504a. Fraudulent Removal of
Leased Property.** (Felony)
Disposing or concealing property purchased under
a contract not yet fulfilled with intent to defraud the
holder of a contract.

Penal Code Section 532a. Making False Statement of Financial Condition. (Misdemeanor)

Any person who knowingly make or causes to be made a statement of his financial condition so that it will be relied upon as being true and correct for the purpose of procuring property (vehicle) knowing the statement to be false.

Penal Code Section 537e. Purchase of Article with the Identification Removed. (Misdemeanor)

Buys, sells, receives, conceals, disposes of, or has in his possession any article with knowledge the identification markings have been removed.

Penal Code Section 538. Removing Mortgaged Personal Property. Concealing or disposing of mortgaged property with intent to defraud the mortgagee.

Penal Code Section 548. Burning Insured Property. (Felony)

Burning a vehicle with intent to defraud an insurance company.

California Vehicle Code Sections:

C.V.C. 4462.b. Improper Display of License Plates and Registration. (Misdemeanor)

Shall not display license plates or registration certificate on a vehicle to which not assigned.

C.V.C. 4463. False Evidence of Registration. (Felony)

Falsification, counterfeit or forged ownership documents or the name of the owner of the vehicle with intent to defraud.

C.V.C. 4464. Altered License Plates. (Misdemeanor)

Altering license plates from their original markings.

C.V.C. 10501. False Report. (Misdemeanor)
Unlawful to make false report of stolen vehicle.

C.V.C. 10502. Embezzled Vehicle Policy.
Embezzled vehicle shall not be broadcast as wanted
until warrant has first been issued.

**C.V.C. 10504. Action by the California Department
of Motor Vehicles.**
Department of Motor Vehicles will maintain a stop
for vehicles reported stolen and embezzled in registration files by license number and by vehicle identification number.

**C.V.C. 10750.a. Altering Vehicle Identification
Numbers.** (Misdemeanor)
Unlawful to alter, deface, or destroy vehicle iden-
tification number.

**C.V.C. 10751. Possession of Vehicle with Identifi-
cation Number Altered.** (Misdemeanor)
Unlawful to buy, sell, receive, possess, or offer for
sale a vehicle whose identification number has been
altered. Must have knowledge number is altered. This
section also includes component parts if they have
identification numbers.

C.V.C. 10851. Theft of Vehicle. (Felony)
Taking a vehicle not his own, without owners consent, with intent to either temporarily or permanently
deprive the owner of his vehicle.

C.V.C. 10852. Tampering with Vehicle. (Misdemeanor)
Unlawful to wilfully tamper with or break a part
of a vehicle or the contents thereof.

C.V.C. 10853. Malicious Mischief of Vehicle. (Misdemeanor)

Unlawful to enter any vehicle with intent to commit malicious mischief, injury, or other crime, nor shall any mechanism be manipulated which would set a vehicle in motion that had been at rest.

C.V.C. 10854. Tampering by Bailee. (Misdemeanor)
Unlawful for bailee to use or tamper with vehicle.

C.V.C. 10855. Leased or Rented Vehicles. (Policy)

Whenever a leased or rented vehicle has not been returned within five days after expiration of the contract, it shall be presumed to have been embezzled.

C.V.C. 11520b. Illegal Wrecking of Vehicles. (Misdemeanor)

Failure to surrender title and license plates to the department of motor vehicle prior to dismantling vehicle.

California Civil Code.

C.C. 3075. Taking Vehicle from Lienholder. (Misdemeanor).

Unlawful to take by trick, fraud, device, a vehicle or parts thereof, from a person holding a lien against that vehicle.

California Insurance Code.

Ins. C. 556 a.
Unlawful to present any false claim for the payment of a loss under a contract of insurance.

Ins. C. 556 b.
Unlawful to prepare any writing with intent the writing will support any fraudulent claim.

The following sections from the California Vehicle Code are not enforcement sections, however, they pertain to the recovery of stolen vehicles.

C.V.C. 2804. Vehicle Inspection.
California Highway Patrol may stop a vehicle to inspect registration.

C.V.C. 2805. Locating Stolen Vehicles.
California Highway Patrol may enter certain business establishments in search of stolen vehicles.

C.V.C. 10850. Application.
The "Anti-Theft" provisions of the California Vehicle Code are applicable upon the highways and elsewhere throughout the State of California.

C.V.C. 22651c. Removal of Vehicles, From Highways.
Any law enforcement officer of the California Highway Patrol, Sheriff's Department or Police department to store for safekeeping in a garage an unattended vehicle from a highway which has been reported stolen or embezzled.

C.V.C. 22653. Removal of Vehicles, Private Property.
Any law enforcement officer of the California Highway Patrol, Sheriff's Department, or Police Department may remove from private property a vehicle which has been reported stolen or embezzled.

C.V.C. 22659c. Removal of Vehicles, State Property.
Authorizes the California State Police to remove stolen or embezzled vehicles from State property to a place of storage.

3

CATEGORIES OF AUTO THIEVES
AND THEIR MODUS OPERANDI

For the most part, auto thieves fall into one of four categories.

1. Temporary Users.
   (Joy Riders)
2. Theft of Vehicles for Parts.
   (Auto Strippers)
3. The Professional Auto Thief.
4. Use of the Stolen Auto in Another Crime.

Temporary Users.

This group accounts for the greatest number of stolen vehicles. Usually the vehicle is taken because transportation is needed. This is common among juveniles who go to a movie, or other diversion, a lengthy distance from their home and stay later than they should, only to find that public transportation has ceased for the day, and no other ride is available, or among members of the armed forces, in need of transportation to return to their base or other destination. This group usually looks for an automobile, any kind will do, which has been parked with the keys left in the ignition. It is driven to within a few blocks of the destination, abandoned there, and usually recovered undamaged.

The automobile today, represents a definite status symbol to the young set. Many youngsters steal autos to drive to school, usually to show off for the day, then abandon them after school. In some cases a thief will steal an auto and hide it to avoid detection and recovery so that he may continue using it for several days. In one such case, a boy of 15 stole a station wagon and drove it to school. During the day and after school, many of his friends were taken for rides in this auto. Later that evening he hid the auto in the garage of a new unoccupied home located in a tract which was under construction. Noting, the following day, that the auto was where he had left it he took the auto and drove it to school again. This practice continued for two weeks before the youth and several of his companions were apprehended driving the auto. This is not an uncommon occurrence.

Parking facilities on and adjacent to school grounds, super market parking lots, parking facilities within apartment complexes, parking areas around military installations and new homes in subdivisions under construction should be given frequent checks for stolen vehicles. Not only are these locations used for the thief to abandon a stolen vehicle, they are target areas for thieves to roam through in search of a vehicle to steal.

The thief who steals an auto for temporary use usually seeks an auto which he can take without any unnecessary delay. He searches for the vehicle whose careless owner left the keys conveniently in the igni-

tion or the ignition in the unlocked position. Hot-
wiring is seldom done by these thieves.

Temporary users, as a rule, are youngsters. They
account for the greatest number of thefts in this cat-
egory. With few exceptions, the stolen auto is seldom
kept more than a day or two. Youngsters late in their
teens, young adults and adults may, in addition to
stealing autos in the locations mentioned earlier, visit
new and used car dealers on the pretext of purchasing
a vehicle and take it for a test drive and not return.

The Auto Stripper.

This person is one who wants something for his
vehicle and either is unable to locate the parts on the
legitimate market or the parts are expensive and he
can not afford to pay for them.

Many automobile parts are difficult to obtain due
to their limited production or because they must be
imported from a foreign country. Still other parts
are very expensive although readily available.

Several years ago it was common for thieves to
steal radios, hub caps, and other such items. Because
engines had identification numbers stamped on the
block, few were taken. Today the complete engine,
transmission, wheels and tires, upholstery, as well as
other parts, may be removed with relatively little
effort. The fact that most of these items are uniden-
tifiable tends to invite their taking. Special "souped-
up" or high performance engines and the four speed
floor shift transmission installed in the regular production American-made sports type and conventional
automobiles by the manufacturer are usually the
targets.

Automobile strippers remove the parts needed for their own use, and remove other parts which they can later sell at "bargain prices" to others. Many of the persons engaged in this activity take orders for certain parts. Then a particular vehicle is stolen, the desired parts are removed and made available to the person who placed the order. Usually the price paid for these items by the receiver is much less than that he would have paid at a legitimate parts dealer, thus enhancing the theft problem. Still others, knowing the popularity of these items, will stock pile four-speed transmissions, bucket seats, special wheels, and certain engines so that they will be on hand when requested by "customers." Hot rod groups and individuals with disreputable reputations who may appear to be engaged in a considerable amount of work on autos deserve frequent checking.

Persons engaged in this activity seek the vehicles needed. They are equipped with the necessary tools to accomplish their objective. Within a matter of a few minutes they can gain entry into a locked vehicle, hot wire the ignition and drive the vehicle to a location where it will be stripped. Many new and used car dealers are "hit" during closed hours. The thief will visit the area where the target vehicle is parked during the business hours and look over the autos in stock. He is looking either for a particular auto to steal or examining the items installed on the autos so that he may return after the dealer has closed and steal them. Having chosen a particular auto to steal, the thief removes a key to it (usually there is more than one key and the dealer will not miss the missing key) and after the dealer has closed, the thief returns and steals the auto. If the thief had marked certain autos to be stripped, he returns and under cover of darkness removes such items as the four speed transmission, engine parts, bucket seats, wheels and tires, and it is often difficult, if not impossible for the police officer on patrol to observe and apprehend the thief in the act of committing the crime. Many of these items can be removed from the auto without raising it off the ground.

Illus. 4

Some vehicles are taken to remote areas and there stripped (Illus. 4). However, others are stripped in well equipped garages, or similar locations, where lights, chain hoist, tools and burning torches are available to strip the vehicle. The vehicle is then pushed away from the garage, usually not far from where it was stripped, and abandoned. Fearing apprehension by the police, the culprits will not run the risk of pushing the vehicle a great distance.

The Professional Auto Thief.

This group's activity attempts to permanently deprive the owner of the possession and use of his vehicle. As in any other business operation, the intention is to make a profit with as little monetary outlay as possible.

One of the most lucrative schemes devised by auto thieves to bilk people out of money, and an activity that has caused many police problems, insofar as recovering vehicles is concerned, is the **vehicle salvage operation.** The operators of this activity are usually well equipped with the means necessary to disguise a vehicle so that its owner would have difficulty identifying it. They are familiar with the requirements for obtaining registration for the altered vehicle and the outlets where the vehicles may be sold. Some of the methods employed by this group are very effective in securing the desired results.

The Totally Wrecked Vehicle — Changing Identification Number.

Probably the most elementary method used is the purchase of a totally wrecked vehicle. Any wrecked vehicle may be purchased from a wrecking yard for this purpose. With the purchase of this vehicle the culprit receives either the title for the vehicle or a bill of sale. Some states allow the license plates to remain with the wrecked vehicle while others require the wrecker to surrender them, together with the title, to the department of motor vehicles. Although in the eyes of law enforcement officials the requirement that both the title and the license plates be surrendered is by far a better policy, neither seems to present an obstacle to the thief, as we will see later. The thief then tows the wrecked vehicle to the place where he is going to work on it. Once inside his garage he removes the vehicle identification number plate (referred to as the V.I.N.) and the license plates if on the vehicle. The wrecked vehicle is then cut into small pieces and hauled off to an iron mill. Any item in good condition, like the engine, other running gear, perhaps a door or the wheels and tires may be saved for future use. Then a vehicle of similar make, body style, and even the color if possible, is stolen. The vehicle identification number plate is removed from the stolen vehicle and in its place the vehicle identification number plate from the wrecked vehicle is installed.

Most vehicle identification number plates are installed by the vehicle manufacturer either with rivets or by spot welding, making their removal difficult and their reuse easy to detect. Some manufacturers, however, use screws to affix the vehicle identification number plate to the body, making their reuse easy. This is common with foreign built vehicles. Further details regarding the vehicle identification number plate will be discussed in a later chapter. The stolen vehicle can then be sold as a rebuilt or revived wreck, using the title obtained from the wrecking company or taking the bill of sale to the motor vehicle department and obtaining a new title.

Few American vehicle engines and transmissions contained an identification number prior to 1968, however, beginning in 1969 most American vehicle engines and other component parts contain numbers identifying the parts to a vehicle. This will require those engaged in the salvage operation to either grind off the identification numbers from parts like the engine and transmission, leaving the obvious sign of attempted obliteration, or remove the parts from the stolen vehicle and install the parts from the wrecked vehicle.

If the vehicle purchased from a wrecking yard is not badly damaged, a vehicle of similar model may be stolen and the necessary parts removed to repair the wrecked vehicle. Here again, all that remains of the stolen vehicle is either abandoned or cut into small pieces and disposed of through an iron mill. Many of the unrecovered stolen vehicles have met their fate in this manner. Cutting the remains into small pieces reduces the possibility of identification and lessens suspicion of both the police and the scrap metal dealer. In addition this junk iron will bring in a few extra dollars.

Alteration of Appearance of Vehicle.

The appearance of stolen vehicles may be altered with little effort. The vehicle may be repainted a different color or color combination; different seat covers may be installed; tires may be changed from black to white or vice versa; locks may be changed. Accessories such as chrome trim, spot lights, hub caps, extra mirrors, radios, and so on, may be removed or installed. Thereafter the title certificate may be forged or the vehicle taken to a non-title state, and by means of a fictitious bill of sale, registered and then sold. In many instances vehicles are taken out of the United States and have found a ready sale.

Fraudulent Purchase.

Another operation, often practiced with expensive vehicles, is to purchase a vehicle from a dealer and make a small down payment or no down payment at all. No alteration to the vehicle is necessary. Title certificates are then forged or counterfeited and the vehicle resold. By the time this trick is discovered, the culprits have struck several dealers, reaped a healthy profit, and moved on to another city or state.

Theft From Automobile Dealers.

This theft presents a particular problem because the thief has been given consent to use the vehicle; and police agencies are reluctant to accept a theft report as this may be referred as an embezzled vehicle. **(Embezzled vehicles will be discussed in chapter 4.)** Usually a reasonable length of time must be allowed for the return of the vehicle. This could vary from a few hours to several days, depending on the circumstances and the attitude of the local district attorney. Knowing this, a thief may plan to be in another city or state within a matter of a few hours, or he may plan to dispose of the vehicle prior to its being placed on the wanted list. Auto rental agencies present similar problems although they may have more information regarding the renter on a rental agreement form which provides the investigating officer with some information to start with.

Check Purchases.

A scheme practiced by both professionals and amateurs is the purchasing of a vehicle with worthless checks. This approach is usually made on the week

end or on holidays when banks are closed and the
check can not be verified. Automobile dealers are seldom the victims for the culprit knows he can not obtain title because the dealer provides the purchaser
with a dealers report of sale, which is only a temporary ownership certificate pending arrival of the per-
manent title, thus allowing the dealer ample time to
verify the check. Therefore the culprit strikes at the
private party who advertises his auto for sale in the
local newspaper. The seller is usually anxious to sell
and the thief does not argue over the price. The
worthless check is given and the title is received. The
thief may now resell the vehicle even for much less
than its value, especially if he is anxious to make
that "fast buck."

The Used Car Dealer's Problem

New and used car dealers often invite some of the
problems they suffer. The professional thief knows
some dealers will purchase any vehicle if "the price is
right." Dealers should be cautioned to exercise care
when purchasing vehicles from unknown persons.

Some practices dealers should guard against:
1. Be suspicious of the person in a hurry to sell
   a vehicle because he is leaving town.
2. Never allow unknown people to take a vehicle
   for a demonstration drive without the salesman. The salesman's presence will assure the
   vehicle's return and prevent having a duplicate key made for later taking of the vehicle.
3. Never allow a vehicle purchased from a private party to remain on the used car lot after
   closing time for several days after the pur-

chase. The former owner may return with a duplicate key, take the vehicle, apply at the motor vehicle department for a duplicate title, and resell the vehicle.

4. When a vehicle is returned from a demonstration drive make certain the keys are returned, and that the keys left in the vehicle are the keys that belong to it **and not ones left in place of the proper keys.**

5. Never take checks from out of town banks, or local banks, from unknown persons when the bank can not be contacted to verify the check.

6. Examine title to the vehicle carefully. Make certain it is for the vehicle involved.

The Trucking Industry, a Prime Target.

A frequent target of the professional thief is the trucking industry with its trucks, truck tractors, and trailers. These vehicles are generally stripped of everything and disposed of over a vast area. Some times the cab and frame may not be reused as these are often identifiable with little effort. Many late model trucks are identifiable by components other than the cab and frame. Almost all parts are useable, either by the thief himself or by the person to whom he has had little trouble selling parts in the past. Parts from these vehicles can be easily sold to "shoe string" trucking firms or truckers who are "just getting by." Their income will not allow expenditures for new parts at legitimate outlets as the parts are expensive.

Motorcycle Thefts.

Motorcycle thefts are similar to the truck thefts in that they can be stripped rapidly and with little effort. Unlike a bulky truck however, which requires a rather large garage in which to be stripped, a motorcycle can be stolen, placed in the rear of a panel truck and stripped or disassembled while enroute to another destination. Parts with identification numbers can be discarded so that only those components without identification marks are retained. These are then repainted and altered in other ways and reused. Members of disreputable motorcycle gangs are known to have a preference for the Harley Davidson motorcycle. Therefore, if a high rate of thefts center around this make of motorcycle, such motorcycle groups should be placed under observation. Other makes of motorcycles, particularly the Honda, Suzuki or the Triumph may be stolen by youngsters for parts and to use off the roadway. Much trading of motorcycle parts is done by these enthusiasts. In addition, off the roadway use of the motor cycle, such as in hill climbs, trail riding, or racing can go unchecked by patrol units. Frequent check of these activities should not be overlooked. In several instances where planned gatherings of disreputable motorcycle groups failed to reveal any motorcycle movement on the roadways enroute to that destination, it was found that members would rent covered or enclosed trailers and transport their motorcycles to the destination so as not to attract the attention of the police.

As a matter of interest, the recovery rate of stolen motorcycles is about 20 percent.

Use of the Stolen Vehicle in Another Crime.

Occasionally a vehicle may be stolen to be used in the commission of another crime. Although this is not a frequent occurance it is a possibility that should not be overlooked. The cases where this would occur are those where the criminal would use the stolen vehicle for transportation in an effort to reduce the possibility of being identified. The type of crime will generally govern what type of vehicle will be stolen, such as an automobile, truck, or trailer. In a recent case, a one and one-half ton van was stolen from a rental agency, during the night when it was closed for business, and the truck used to haul thirty colored television sets away from a furniture store which was burglarized. It is obvious that in this case transportation for the television sets were needed.

4

VEHICLE EMBEZZLEMENT

Vehicle embezzlement is difficult to investigate because it is not really a clear-cut crime. The main difference between embezzlement and theft is that if an embezzlement, the victim has given someone permission to use the vehicle, whereas in theft, usually no permission is granted. In order to provide the victim with the best possible attention to his problem, the police officer should initiate the investigation as he would any other crime.

Embezzlement Defined.

Embezzlement is defined in Section 503 of the California Penal Code as "The fraudulent appropriation of property by a person to whom it is entrusted."

Some methods used by those who practice vehicle embezzlement are described in the following case histories:

Case #1.

An individual advertises his vehicle for sale in the local newspaper over a weekend. A prospective buyer calls to look at the vehicle. After test driving it, the culprit decides to purchase it and gives the seller a check for the price asked for the vehicle. There may or may not be any discussion over the price; as a matter of fact, a culprit experienced in this racket will argue a little over the price in an effort to get the seller to reduce it. The victim then endorses the ownership certificate and gives it to the buyer along with the vehicle. The buyer then goes to a used car dealer, title in hand, and sells the vehicle. The culprit has obtained cash for the vehicle, and it will be a day or two before the original owner learns from the bank that the check given him is worthless.

Case #2.

Culprit borrows a vehicle, most often from a friend but anyone who will lend him one will do, and goes to a Department of Motor Vehicles office where, claiming he lost the ownership documents for the vehicle, he makes application for duplicate ownership documents, forging the rightful owner's name but using a different address. Vehicle is then returned to the owner and the culprit awaits receipt of the duplicate title. When he receives it, culprit again borrows the same vehicle and sells it.

Case #3.

Culprit goes to an automobile dealer late in the evening or over a weekend wanting to purchase a particular vehicle. He gives the salesman a fictitious name and other credit information in order to obtain financing so that he will not be required to give any of his own money. This also lessens the possibility of the salesman's becoming **suspicious because the culprit wants to pay the total price by check.** The down payment, usually very small, however, is paid for with a worthless check, the vehicle is delivered to the culprit, and it is many days or weeks before the automobile dealer learns the transaction was a bad one. By this time the vehicle can be driven to a non-title state where, by use of a fictitious bill of sale, title can be obtained. The vehicle is then driven to another state and sold.

Another use for a vehicle obtained in this fashion is to strip it of parts needed for another similar vehicle.

Case #4.

Culprit rents a vehicle from a rental agency for a day or two. He uses a stolen or fraudulently obtained credit card, along with false identification, to charge the rental fee. The vehicle is never returned.

Case #5.

Culprit contracts to rent a vehicle for a day or two, using his true name, and pays the minimum required deposit fee in cash. Usually a particular vehicle is rented — one for which there is a need. The culprit then strips the rented vehicle of the items he needs to install in another similar vehicle. The rented vehicle is then reported stolen, and when recovered in a stripped condition, the insurance company is forced to repair the rented vehicle, and the culprit will have obtained the parts he needs for only a few dollars.

Case #6.

Culprit goes to an automobile dealer and asks to take a vehicle out for a test drive. He is allowed to test drive a vehicle and fails to return. Similarly, culprit answers advertisement of a vehicle for sale in a newspaper by a private party and does the same thing.

When there is a Case of Embezzlement.

The above methods are cited to illustrate a few of the problems encountered by the police as well as the victims. Police officers are reluctant to take action, but the victim wants his property returned, of course. California Vehicle Code Section 10502 states in part ". . . but in the event of an embezzlement may make the report only after having procured the issuance of a warrant for the arrest of the person charged with such embezzlement." And Section 10855 of the California Vehicle Code states "Whenever any person has leased or rented a vehicle wilfully and intentionally fails to return the vehicle to its owner within five days after the lease or rental agreement has expired, the person shall be presumed to have embezzled the vehicle."

Most departments will allow an officer to make his investigation in an effort to determine if a crime has been committed, but in the case of embezzlement it must be submitted to the district attorney for review, and then, only after a complaint has been authorized and a warrant issued for someone's arrest, will the vehicle be placed in the wanted file. Should the district attorney rule that the case does not contain the elements necessary for criminal prosecution the victim should be advised to pursue the matter through civil channels.

5

THE STOLEN VEHICLE REPORT

Beginning the Investigation.

An auto theft investigation is usually set into motion by the owner, or the person who is in control of the vehicle, upon discovery that the vehicle is missing. The victim calls the police department to report the loss. The officer responding to investigate must question the victim regarding the loss in an effort to determine three important factors:

1. Whether a crime has in fact been committed, i.e., the officer must be reasonably certain the vehicle was stolen.
2. Whether it is a civil matter.
3. Whether it is a false reporting such as an intoxicated person attempting to cover up a hit-run accident.

Two important considerations which w o u l d definitely change a reported theft from a criminal matter to a civil matter are:

1. Who is the legal owner?
   a. Whether or not the vehicle is being purchased under an installment contract and who the finance company is.
   b. Whether the payments are current.
   c. Whether the vehicle was repossessed.

Should it appear, from talking to the victim, that possibly the finance company repossessed the vehicle, the report may be taken. However, this avenue MUST BE INVESTIGATED PRIOR TO ANY STEPS BEING TAKEN TO BROADCAST THE VEHICLE AS STOLEN on any form of an all points bulletin. This responsibility rests with the police officer. If it is determined that the vehicle was repossessed, the owner should be informed as soon as possible and the theft report correctly labelled and cancelled.

2. The investigating officer must determine that the vehicle is not in the possession of anyone who could have legal possession of it, such as another member of the family or an estranged spouse.

With these questions answered to the satisfaction of the officer, he then has reasonable cause to believe the crime of auto theft has been committed, and may proceed to question the victim regarding the circumstances surrounding the disappearance of the vehicle. It is here that records of the frequency of past thefts in the area will be beneficial to the officer as he proceeds with the investigation.

Preparation of the Report.

Preparing a report on the theft of a motor vehicle does not differ from any other crime report insofar as what information is to be recorded. The WHAT, WHERE, WHEN, WHO, HOW, and WHY information should be obtained as accurately and as completely as possible. Sample of Auto Theft report forms used by various police departments are illustrated by illustrations 5-9.

The officer will want to determine as much of the following information as possible. Remember, the first contact with the victim is always the best contact.

STOLEN ☐	EMBEZZLED ☐

Specify Type of Report by Marking with "X"

Department Reporting	Area or Division	Date	File Number

DESCRIPTION OF VEHICLE

Year Make Model	Body Type	Year State License No.	Color Combination, Exterior
Vehicle Identification Number (VIN)	Engine Number (EN)	Type Transmission	Color Combination, Interior
Other Identifying Marks		Type Hub Caps	Spot Lights

Registered Owner	Address	City	State	Phone Number
Legal Owner	Address	City	State	Phone Number

CIRCUMSTANCES SURROUNDING OCCURRENCE

Location of Occurrence	Time and Date Stolen
Person Reporting Occurrence	Address	City	Phone No.	Time and Date Reported

Doors Locked?	Ignition Locked?	If Insured, Name of Company	Payments Current?	Last Driver of Vehicle
Has Embezzlement Warrant Been Issued?	Warrant No.	Court?		

DESCRIPTION OF SUSPECTS

Name	Address	City	Sex	Age	Ht.	Wt.	Hair	Eyes	Operator's License No.

METHOD OF OPERATION

Include Names, Addresses and Comments of Persons Contacted for Additional Information

AFFIRMATION

I, the undersigned, do hereby certify that to the best of my knowledge the information given on this form is true and accurate.

Signature of Person Making Stolen Report	Signature of Officer or Employee Taking or Making Report
Date	Title	I.D. No.

CHP 180 (REV. 6)

Illus. 5.
Report form of the California Highway Patrol.

Thereafter facts are not as clear, other influences may have an effect on the victims judgment, or he may leave the area either temporarily or permanently.

P. D. Form 86A 3-67

Report No._____

Police Department, City of Sacramento

REPORT OF MOTOR VEHICLE - STOLEN ☐ **RECOVERED** ☒ **IMPOUNDED** ☐ **STORED** ☐

Complainant/Owner_____
Address_____ Phone_____
Business Address_____ Business Phone_____
When stolen/recovered/impounded, Date_____ Hour_____
Where stolen/recovered/impounded_____
Reported by_____ Address_____ Phone_____
Reported to: Officer_____ Date_____ Hour_____

Description of Vehicle:

Make_____ VIN No._____ Mtr. No._____
Type_____ Year Model_____ Color_____ No. Cylinders_____
License No._____ Year_____ State_____
Registered Owner_____ Address_____
Legal Owner_____ Address_____
Condition of vehicle when recovered/impounded/ (Good, stripped, etc.)_____
Out of gas, keys missing, etc._____ Okeh to release_____
Disposition of vehicle (Garage, to owner, etc.)_____

If Vehicle Impounded or Stored - Reason:

Reported stolen_____ Traffic collision_____ Traffic hazard_____ Abandoned_____ Evidence_____ Other_____
Person arrested/cited: Name_____ Charge_____

If Vehicle Stolen:

Locks in use: Ignition_____ Doors_____ Insured With_____
Broadcast_____ Cancelled_____
Auto Status Sent_____ Cancelled_____
Warrant vs._____ Charge_____ Date_____
Connect-ups: Report Nos._____

CLEARANCE:

Person Arrested_____
Cleared (Indicate how)_____
Cleared by (Name and Star No.)_____ Div/Detail_____ Date_____

Vehicle Recovered:

Where recovered_____ Date_____
Reported stolen from_____ Date_____ Report No._____
Recovery by (Name and Star No.)_____ Div/Detail_____ Date_____

DETAILS (If stolen vehicle, state size, make and serial number of tires, list accessories, description and value of property in vehicle etc.)

Release and Waiver:

Know all men by these presents: That I,_____

of the City of_____ County of_____ State of California, do by these presents, for myself, my heirs, administrators or assigns, release each, every and all duly appointed Peace Officers of any city, county or city and county of the State of California, or of the California Highway Patrol of the State of California, from any claim, action, demands, dues, sums of money, controversies, trespasses, judgments, executions, claims and demands whatsoever, in law or in equity, I ever had or now have or which I, or my heirs, executors, administrators or assigns, hereafter can, shall or may have against any Peace Officer or Peace Officers recovering, holding, storing, or conveying, the above described vehicle, which I have this day reported as stolen and which is now not in my possession. This release and waiver will remain in effect until such time as above described vehicle shall be recovered and again be in my possession.

Is vehicle community property?_____ Are you delinquent in payments?_____

SIGNATURE OF PERSON MAKING REPORT_____

SIGNED, OFFICER_____ Date_____ Hour_____

Ill.

Illus. 6.

Report form of the City of Sacramento Police Department.

AUTOMOBILE THEFT REPORT
POLICE DEPARTMENT — CITY OF MINNEAPOLIS

REPORT NUMBER

Verified MVB
Dispatcher Notified
TWX No.
Cancelled - TWX No.

LICENSE   MOTOR   SERIAL   MODEL

MAKE   TYPE   COLOR OF BODY   SPEEDOMETER READING

MAKE OF TIRES   SPARE TIRE & WHEEL   RADIO   VALUE OF CAR $

OTHER EQUIPMENT (LIST SPOT LAMPS, REAR VIEW MIRROR, ETC.)

IDENTIFYING CHARACTERISTICS

PERSONAL PROPERTY IN CAR

OWNER   PERSON REPORTING

ADDRESS   ADDRESS

TELEPHONE: RES.   BUS.   TELEPHONE: RES.   BUS.

DATE OF THEFT   19   HOURS   DAY OF WEEK   CENSUS TRACT #   OR BETWEEN   DATE   HOURS   AND   DATE   HOURS

CAR WAS PARKED AT   ON STREET - ALLEY - PARKING LOT - USED CAR LOT - GARAGE - YARD

DOORS LOCKED?   IGNITION LOCKED?   WHERE ARE KEYS?

WHERE WAS OWNER/ATTENDANT AT TIME OF THEFT?   WILL OWNER PROSECUTE?   SUSPECT ANYONE?

IF SO, DESCRIBE AND STATE REASONS FOR SUSPICION

DID OWNER/ATTENDANT PERMIT ANYONE TO USE CAR?   UNDER WHAT CONDITIONS?

ABSOLUTE OWNERSHIP?   FINANCE CO.   INSURANCE CO.

I HEREBY CERTIFY THAT THE FOREGOING STATEMENT IS TRUE AND CORRECT

REPORT RECEIVED BY   TELEPHONE / IN PERSON   DATE   19 .   HRS

REMARKS:

DATE RECOVERED   19 .   HRS   IMPOUNDED AT   19 .   HRS

WHERE RECOVERED   OWNER NOTIFIED BY

RECOVERED BY   DATE OF NOTICE   19 .   HRS

ARRESTS

Illus. 7.
Report form of the city of Minneapolis, Minnesota, Police Department.

Form 3a—20M—11-65   SP*25906-357

TIME ......8:00 P.M.......   OFFICER'S REPORT   No. ....

                                          OREGON STATE POLICE

Place   ..Medford ....   County ....Marion................................

Subject   RECOVERED AUTO..............   ....June 29....................., 1966..

'62 Chev. Sdn. Ore. 4N-6005, ID #1122334

Reg. Owner - ROE, JOHN G., 1222 Main Street, Salem, Oregon

Refer - APB SMO 140 6-28-66

DOE, JOHN RAY - Accused

  Vehicle recovered at 4:00 A.M. this date near Medford on
Hwy. I-5.

  John Ray Doe, OSB #1234, WM, DOB 6-10-44, 5'10", 170 lbs., brown
hair, blue eyes, 1234 East Main Street, Salem, Oregon was arrested and
admitted theft - see attached statement.

  Vehicle stored at Jones Garage, Medford, Oregon in running
condition.

  Cleared by radio and APB 170 at 4:20 A.M., 6-29-66

     613-31 JOHN LAWMAN, Pfc.

Illus. 8.
Officer's report form of the Oregon State Police.

What Happened — Description of Vehicle.

What was taken?

All theft reports must be headed with the specific
type of offense. This answers what happened. Insofar
as crime reporting is concerned, it is usually easy to
describe what was taken but the check list of items
1 through 11 which follow will serve as memory
joggers.

  1. Year model of the vehicle.

  2. Make of vehicle and name of the model, i.e.,
   Ford: Galaxie, Thunderbird, Mustang, Ran-
   chero; Chevrolet: Impala, Corvette, Camaro,
   El Camino.

  3. Body style.
   Be specific and describe the body exactly. 2

ONTARIO PROVINCIAL POLICE

VEHICLE REPORT FORM

1. REGISTERED OWNER'S NAME (SURNAME, GIVEN NAMES) | 2. LICENCE NO.
21. PERSON LAST DRIVING VEHICLE | 3. REGISTERED OWNER'S ADDRESS CITY | YEAR PROV. TYPE
22. DRIVER'S ADDRESS CITY | 4. PHONE-RES/BUS. | 5. TYPE OF VEHICLE | 6. GHQ FILE NO.
23. DRIVER'S PHONE RES/BUS | 24. SOBRIETY ☐ SBR. ☐ HBD. ☐ INTX | 7. MOTOR SERIAL NUMBER | 8. VEHICLE IDENT. NUMBER | 9. DET. (NAME AND CODE)
25. DRIVER'S OCCUPATION, SEX, RACE, AGE | 10. YEAR MAKE MODEL STYLE COLOUR(S) | 11. DET FILE NO.
26. VEHICLE INSURED BY PHONE | 12. LIEN HOLDER/FINANCED BY | 13. DHQ FILE NO.
27. RADIO MESSAGE ☐ YES ☐ NO TIME DATE | 14. NATURE OF OCCURRENCE | 15. TIME/DATE REPORTED | 16. TELETYPE NO.
28. WARRANT ☐ YES ☐ NO AREA OF RETURN | 17. STOLEN OR TAKEN FROM (ADDRESS OR LOCATION) CITY | 18. TIME/DATE STOLEN/TAKEN
29. IF TOWED - GARAGE NAME | 19. RECOVERED FROM (ADDRESS) CITY | 20. TIME/DATE RECOVERED
30. GARAGE ADDRESS CITY | 31. STORED AT | 32. OWNER NOTIFIED ☐ YES ☐ NO (EXPLAIN)
33. REPORTED BY ☐ OWNER ☐ DRIVER ☐ OTHER | IF OTHER: NAME ADDRESS CITY PHONE NO. RES./BUS.

34. IGNITION LOCKED ☐ YES ☐ NO | 35. KEYS IN IGNITION ☐ YES ☐ NO | 36. DOORS LOCKED ☐ YES ☐ NO | 37. WINDOWS CLOSED ☐ YES ☐ NO | 38. TRUNK LOCKED ☐ YES ☐ NO | 39. POWER STEERING ☐ YES ☐ NO
40. POWER WINDOWS ☐ YES ☐ NO | 41. POWER BRAKES ☐ YES ☐ NO | 42. POWER SEATS ☐ YES ☐ NO | 43. ADJ. STEERING WHEEL ☐ YES ☐ NO | 44. RADIO IN VEHICLE ☐ YES ☐ NO | 45. BATTERY IN VEHICLE ☐ YES ☐ NO
46. SPARE TIRE IN VEHICLE ☐ YES ☐ NO | 47. OWNERSHIP IN VEHICLE ☐ YES ☐ NO | 48. TRANSMISSION - TYPE | 49. MILEAGE | 50. VALUE OF VEHICLE $ | 51. VALUE OF CONTENTS $
52. REPAINTED ☐ YES ☐ NO IF YES, STATE ORIGINAL COLOUR | 53. IDENTIFIABLE MARKS OR DAMAGE TO VEHICLE
54. IDENTIFIABLE ACCESSORIES OR PROPERTY IN VEHICLE (SPECIFY MAKE, MODEL, ETC.)

55. IDENTIFY SUSPECTS BY NO. NAME-ADDRESS-SEX-RACE-AGE-HT-WT-HAIR-EYES-COMPL-CLOTHING-IDENTIFYING CHARACTERISTICS. (IF ARRESTED, INCLUDE NAME-ADDRESS-SEX-RACE-DATE OF BIRTH-PRISONER IDENTIFICATION NO. AND CHARGE.)
(1)
(2)

STOLEN VEHICLE RECOVERY
56. BY WHOM RECOVERED (NAME AND RANK OF OFFICER, AND NAME OF POLICE DEPT. - IF CITIZEN, NAME, ADDRESS, PHONE NO.)
57. LOCATION OF RECOVERY | 58. METHOD OF THEFT (JUMP WIRES-TIN FOIL-IGNITION-LEFT OPEN ETC.)
59. DESCRIBE EVIDENCE OF STRIPPING, TAMPERING | 60. IDENT. TECHNICIAN AT SCENE (NAME OR REASON NOT CALLED)

ITEM NO. | 61. NARRATIVE: (1) IDENTIFY ADDITIONAL SUSPECTS (2) IDENTIFY WITNESSES BY NAME, ADDRESS AND TELEPHONE NUMBERS (3) DESCRIBE PHYSICAL EVIDENCE LEFT AT SCENE OF THEFT OR IN OR NEAR RECOVERED CAR (4) SUMMARIZE DETAILS OF OCCURRENCE AND INVESTIGATION. (5) LIST ANY PERTINENT OR VALUABLE ITEMS IN CAR WHEN STOLEN AND/OR RECOVERED. FOR ADDITIONAL SPACE USE SUPPLEMENTARY REPORT.

62. CIRCULAR ☐ YES ☐ NO | 63. BULLETIN ☐ YES ☐ NO | 64. CIRCULATION AREA ☐ DIST. ☐ PROV. | 65. RECOMMENDED BY (DET. COMMANDER) ☐ YES ☐ NO | 66. APPROVED BY (SUPERINTENDENT) ☐ YES ☐ NO
67. CASE STATUS ☐ UNFOUNDED ☐ CLEARED BY CHARGE ☐ CLEARED OTHERWISE (EXPLAIN IN NARRATIVE) | 68. REPORT STATUS | 69. REPORT SUBMITTED BY NAME NUMBER RANK DATE
70. APPROVED BY (DET. COMMANDER) NAME RANK | 71. REVIEWED BY (GHQ USE) NAME DATE | 72. APPROVED FOR FILING (GHQ USE) NAME DATE

Illus. 9.
Vehicle report form of the Ontario (Canada) Provincial Police.

door and 4 door models are available in sedans, convertibles, station wagons, and pickup trucks. Trailers should include the number of axles, type and size of the bed.

4. Color or color combination.

5. License number.
   State from which the license plate was issued
   and the year. Are both plates displayed on the
   vehicle?

6. Vehicle Identification Number.
   Exercise care in writing numbers and letters
   in order that they are misunderstood; i.e.,
   5 for S, 2 for Z, etc.

7. Keys left in the ignition switch.
   Were the keys left in the ignition switch or
   was the ignition switch left in the "off" position rather than in the "locked" position. Few
   1969 model vehicles and most of the 1970 model
   vehicles came equipped with a steering column
   locking devise which locked the steering column and the gear shifting mechanism. With
   the ignition switch locked the vehicle can not
   be rolled as the shift lever on a vehicle with
   an automatic transmission locks in the park
   position and the vehicle with a standard transmission locks in the reverse position. In addition, the steering shaft locks so the front
   wheels can not be turned. To insure the most
   efficiency from this device, it was designed so
   the key could not be removed unless the shifting lever was either in the park or reverse
   positions and a buzzer sounds until the key is
   removed from the lock. (Illus. 10 and Illus. 11).

8. Number of keys.
   How many keys does the victim have for the
   vehicle and can he account for ALL of them.

9. Special equipment.
   List special equipment the vehicle came
   equipped with from the factory or extra equip-

Illus. 10
Position of ignition switch which
can be operated without a key.

Illus. 11
1970 Ford steering column lock.

ment added to the vehicle. Include such items
as:
    a. Special racing engine.
    b. Four-speed transmission.
    c. Magnesium, magnesium t y p e or chrome
wheels.
    d. Racing tires.
    e. Bucket seats.
    f. Other accessory or modification.
  10. Personal articles.
    Personal articles left in the interior or the
trunk of the vehicle.
  11. Unusual features.
    List any unusual features which may help iden-
tify the vehicle such as:
    a. Dents or scratches.
    b. Broken or cracked glass. (include lamp
lenses).
    c. Missing parts.

12. Other Facts to be Ascertained or Determined.

In addition to describing the stolen vehicle, check
for the following:
    a. What evidence, if any, was found at the

location from where the vehicle was stolen?

b. What did the victim do upon discovering his vehicle missing?

c. Did he contact anyone? If he did, who was it?

d. What other crime appears to have been committed?
Burglary.
Robbery.
Grand or Petty Theft.

e. What is the officers appraisal of the character of the victim?

f. What follow-up investigation will be required of the auto theft investigators?

g. What other agencies or details should be informed of this theft?

  i. Local police agencies.

  ii. State Police or Highway Patrol (attention to their commercial enforcement facilities—particularly on truck thefts)

  iii. Neighboring states.

  iv. Federal Bureau of Investigation.

  v. State border inspection stations.

  vi. Forgery or Bad Check Detail.

  vii. Burglary Detail.

  viii. Narcotics Detail.

  ix. Pawn Shop Detail.

Where Did It Happen?

Where was the crime committed?

This is simply the geographic location from where the vehicle was stolen. It may be a garage or home from which an address can be obtained. It may be a roadway where only the name of the street is available. Indicate on the report, when possible, the direction the vehicle was facing when the victim left it parked. This may be a useful clue to establish flight and helps in plotting thefts on pin maps.

After the officer has taken the theft report and is finished interviewing the victim and witnesses, he should check the area where the vehicle was stolen for any stolen vehicles that may have been abandoned there. Any stolen vehicles recovered in the area should be examined for evidence. An effort should be made to see if there is a connection between the recovered vehicle and the most recent theft in that area.

Where was the victim when the vehicle was stolen?

Where were the witnesses?

Where is the evidence stored?

When Did It Happen?

When was the vehicle first discovered missing?
1. Date
2. Time

When was the theft reported to the police?
1. Date
2. Time

Unlike most other crimes it is sometimes very difficult, if not impossible to accurately pin point the exact hour or even day when a vehicle was stolen. Having parked his vehicle, there is no one to know that there is anything amiss until the owner returns and makes the discovery for himself. Some typical examples would be the vacationer who returns home after an absence of days or weeks to discover his loss, or the next door neighbor who parks his car at the curb overnight only to find it gone in the morning.

A more difficult situation is an automobile dealer who discovers a vehicle missing upon taking inventory. He is faced with the problem of determining if it is being used by an employee or a customer, if it is being repaired or if it has been sold. Therefore, the report should indicate the time and date the vehicle was last seen, and the time and date the theft was discovered.

Example: Vehicle was parked west bound in front of 700 - 54th Street, Sacramento, Calif. at 9:30 P.M. on 1-24-70 and discovered missing at 8:00 A.M. on 1-24-70.

Should there be an unreasonable lapse between the time of the discovery of the theft and the time the theft was reported to the police, the reason should be ascertained and included in the report. In addition, there must be a reason when the theft is reported by someone other than the owner of the vehicle. This too should be explained in the report.

Who is the Victim — the Suspect?

The victim is the one against whom the crime is committed, or the one who suffers a loss. He has the right to report the theft; even though he may not be the owner. When someone other than the owner files a theft report, that person's relationship with the owner as well as the name of the owner and his whereabouts should be indicated in the report. The victim may only be able to furnish the officer a description of the vehicle and where he last observed it.

Rarely will he be able to supply any information regarding the theft or suspects.

1. The victim should be completely identified; and this information should include his address, where he is employed, and telephone number for each.

2. Is the victim the owner of the vehicle?

If not, by what authority does he claim possession of the vehicle?

The vehicle may have been loaned to the victim by a friend or it may be a loaner from a garage. It may also be a vehicle leased by the victim from an auto leasing agency.

3. Who is the registered owner of the vehicle?

The registered owner is the firm or person who has an interest in a vehicle, but who cannot receive clear and complete title to the vehicle until a security interest held by another is satisfied.

4. Who is the legal owner of the vehicle?

The legal owner is the person or firm who holds a security trust (mortgage or lien) on a vehicle, or the complete clear title to the vehicle.

5. Who is the lessor?

The lessor is one in the business of leasing vehicles.

6. Who is the lessee?

The lessee is one who leased the vehicle.

7. Who is reporting the theft?

8. Who has been interviewed?

Obtain complete identity for future contact or for service of subpoena.

9. Who assisted with the investigation?
   a. Name
   b. Departmental identification number
   c. Agency, Department or Detail

10. Who discovered the theft?
11. Who will conduct the follow-up investigation?
12. Who will file the complaint?
13. Who is the witness?

Is he willing to testify; and will he make a competent witness in court? A witness is only as good as the information he possesses, and his ability and willingness to testify as to what he knows clearly and with certainty in a court of law.

14. Identify all witnesses and request that they inform you should they move, go on vacation, or leave the area for any other reason.

15. Who is a suspect?

Any information that can be developed to indicate a suspect should be included in the report with as much detail as possible.

17. Who was the last driver prior to the theft of the vehicle?

18. Who is the insurance company?

Investigating officers may want to contact the insurance company representative regarding the theft. Insurance adjusters are very helpful and can obtain statements from the victim and witnesses in addition to those obtained by the officers. These should be compared for discrepancies in cases where a false report is made in an attempt to defraud the insurance company.

19. Who is the agency (reporting department) reporting the theft?

This is the department who issues the All Points Bulletin which broadcasts the theft of a vehicle and any suspects as wanted.

How Was the Vehicle Stolen?

1. Was the vehicle locked in a garage; or had it been left in the street unlocked and with the keys in the ignition.

2. Was the garage door pried open in order to steal the vehicle?

3. How was entry gained into the vehicle?

4. How did the thief arrive at the location where the theft occurred?

5. Was another vehicle used to tow the stolen vehicle away?

6. How was the theft discovered?

Why Was the Vehicle Stolen?

Generally the answer to why the vehicle was stolen will not be learned until the vehicle is recovered, or the thief apprehended. However, a good bet will be that someone wanted it for transportation, for stripping, or for altering and reselling.

6

DISSEMINATING STOLEN VEHICLE INFORMATION

Desirability of Speedy Dissemination of Information.

After gathering as much information about the theft as possible, and as soon after the theft as possible, the department taking the report should broadcast the information by police, teletype facilities, and any other means available to apprise other agencies of the theft.

It is important that this information be made available to other officers within the department, as well as to officers of other agencies as soon as possible. There are several reasons for this. First, a speedy recovery engenders good relations with the victim; and this type of publicity is accepted favorably by the public. And, of course, the thief must be apprehended without incident, if possible. Most important, however, all officers on duty must be aware the vehicle is stolen and possibly occupied by criminals. Should the stolen vehicle be observed, officers then will take the necessary precautions to avoid injury to themselves in capturing the culprits, and recovery of the vehicle, undamaged if possible.

Methods of Transmitting Information.

Generally there are four methods of transmitting the stolen vehicle information:

1. Police radio broadcast for local departments.
2. Police teletype systems for statewide and neighboring states (All Points Bulletins).
3. Police bulletins — flyer information usually mailed to agencies of other states with wanted vehicle information.
4. Police computerized information systems.

Police radio broadcasts and all points bulletins (APB's) should not be lengthy, but should include the following information:

Year of the vehicle.

Vehicle make.

Model of the vehicle make.

Color or color combination.

Body style.

License plate number including year and state issued.

Vehicle identification number (VIN).

Names of any suspects.

Complete descriptions of suspects.

Whether or not warrants of arrest have been issued for the suspects.

Possible destination of the suspects or the vehicle if known.

If apprehended out of state, will the department extradite.

Name of agency and case number.

For those departments that are decentralized — those having district offices, area offices, or precinct stations — the office originating the message should be identified in order that anyone desiring to communicate with the originator will know where to direct his message.

As additional information is developed through follow-up investigation, supplemental information should be issued.

Cancellation of Reports Upon Recovery of Vehicle.

Just as it is important to issue information relating to a stolen vehicle, it is equally important to cancel it when the vehicle has been recovered and the suspect apprehended or the suspect is no longer wanted. Undesirable criticism, an illegal arrest, or an unjustified injury could result when a wanted vehicle, having actually been recovered, is not removed from the wanted list.

National Crime Information Center.

The National Crime Information Center (NCIC) is a computerized information system that was established at Federal Bureau of Investigation Headquarters, Washington, D.C., in January 1967 as a service to all law enforcement agencies — local, state and federal. The system operates by means of computers. Data is transmitted over communication lines to agencies equipped with facilities tied to this system. The service provided by NCIC is available twenty four hours a day, seven days a week.

The objective of the NCIC system is to improve the effectiveness of law enforcement through the more efficient handling and exchange of documented police information. Data stored in the NCIC and access to it is restricted to authorized law enforcement agencies only. All the information contained in the NCIC has been contributed by the many police agencies tied to this system. It is not the sole workings of any one department.

Eventually when all fifty states are tied to this system, the NCIC will serve as an index for all law enforcement information systems. Such a centralized crime information system in each state would provide a potent instrument for the police to use in the continuing battle in the suppression of criminal acts. The state agency operating the centralized statewide system will then be a control terminal in the NCIC system.

Information and records stored in the NCIC file include the following:

Wanted persons.

Stolen vehicles (cars, trucks, trailers, motorcycles).

Stolen aircraft.

Vehicles wanted in connection with a felony crime.

Stolen license plates. If the stolen plates are from a state issuing two plates for a vehicle then both plates have to be stolen before they can be entered in NCIC. One stolen plate by itself cannot be entered if the other plate is available. If only one plate is issued for the vehicle and it is stolen then this plate can be entered as stolen.

Stolen, missing or recovered guns.

Stolen articles that can be identified by serial number. This includes vehicle engines and transmissions if they have identifying numbers as well as radios, televisions, cameras, and so on.

Stolen, missing, or embezzled securities, stocks, bonds, currency, and so on.

Loaned, rented, or leased vehicles can be entered into NCIN provided a complaint has been issued charging a crime has been committed.

Stolen boats.

It is the responsibility of the agency initiating a message to assure its accuracy and to up-date the information as needed. The originating agency is also responsible for the cancellation of that message when an apprehension or recovery is made. Insuring that such cancellations are made is of vital importance.

Automatic Statewide Auto Theft Inquiry System.

For many years, the California Highway Patrol has been required, by statute, to maintain a state wide auto theft file. Prior to 1963, almost all California police departments maintained their own individual wanted vehicle file as well. This resulted in considerable duplication and, what was worse, inaccurate or incomplete information. Realizing the serious auto theft problem faced in California, several police agencies conducted a study in an effort to develop a system of collecting the information and making this information available to all California police agencies from a central depository. Finally, in April of 1963, after surmounting many hurdles, California's Automatic Statewide Auto Theft Inquiry System, better known as "Auto-Statis," was placed in operation at the California Highway Patrol Headquarters in Sacramento. This system serves all police agencies in California, as well as other states, including Hawaii, as they tie into the system.

To further facilitate rapid access to information, the Auto-Statis system was interfaced with the F.B.I.'s NCIC system in 1967. Additionally the California Department of Justice (DOJ) also interfaced with the systems, the total of which provides the California police officer with the largest, most complete file of stolen and wanted vehicles, persons and property in the United States on a twenty four hour a day, seven day a week basis.

There is no doubt that the automated system of storing and disseminating information is by far superior to former methods used. However, information provided the police officer by this system must be evaluated with other facts known by the officer at the scene. When a positive response (a hit) is received, the officer should take those steps necessary to assure the want is currently valid. Likewise a negative response (not wanted) should not preclude any additional inquiry of other sources. It must be remembered that computers are machines and the information they store is fed them by people. All such systems should be considered as informational tools — not substitutes for the officer's professional police judgment.

7

WHAT TO LOOK FOR IN
A STOLEN VEHICLE

Initial Contact with a Stolen Vehicle.

As a rule, officers assigned to traffic enforcement are in the best position to look for and come in contact with stolen vehicles. And in most cases this contact will be made with the stolen vehicle in motion and occupied by the thieves. Careful attention will result in the officer's making this contact with maximum safety, insuring the apprehension of the thieves and the recovery of the vehicle without incident.

Officers assigned to patrol duty usually encounter the stolen vehicle while it is parked or abandoned. Patrol officers should maintain surveillance on the areas where abandoned stolen vehicles are being recovered as well as the locations where thefts are reported with high frequency. Officers should check persons loitering around these "trouble spots" in an effort to reduce the thefts and tampering.

The Time and Place of Theft.

Most vehicles are stolen because careless motorists leave their cars unlocked, keys in the ignition switch, or leave the ignition switch in the unlocked position, thus inviting a thief to steal the vehicle. Many of these vehicles will be gone for some time before the loss is discovered and police called. There will be an additional time lapse, although this should be a very short period, during which the police will be investigating the report to determine the authenticity of the theft. Naturally the thief will not always know how soon the vehicle will be discovered missing and the police alerted. From the time he takes the vehicle, the thief will attempt to cover up his crime in an effort to go unnoticed. With this in mind, the thief may take a vehicle during the late evening hours or early morning hours, from either the street or a car dealer's lot. This is almost sure to give him eight hours, or even more, before the crime is discovered and reported to the police. The thief who finds a vehicle parked during the day with the keys in the ignition switch may not have more than an hour or so, if this much, before the theft is discovered and the police alerted. For this reason both the traffic and patrol officers must be constantly on the alert for the thief and the stolen vehicle.

Recognition of Stolen Vehicles.

The following hints are suggested as a guide to assist officers in recognizing stolen vehicles:

1. Upon reporting for duty, check the stolen vehicle "hot sheet" prepared by the department and, if possible, carry one during tour of duty.

2. Do not rely on the "hot sheet" entirely. Check with the radio dispatcher regarding suspected vehicles not on "hot sheet."

3. License plates should not be relied upon as

being accurate identification for the vehicle. Cold license plates may easily be substituted for hot license plates. Where possible, always refer to the vehicle identification number (VIN) to check the vehicle for wants. Refer to illustration in chapter 11 for the various locations of vehicle identification number plates affixed to vehicles.

4. Look for signs of forced entry, broken wind wing glass (either right or left side). (Illus 12.) Chipped edge of wind wing glass near latch.

   Pry marks on door glass channel or trunk lid. Locked vehicles may easily be entered through some wind wing or other glass areas. If the glass is broken it is readily noticeable; however, a smart or experienced thief may remove the broken glass altogether, and from a distance its absence is not noticeable. (Illus 13.)

Illus. 12	Illus. 13
Shattered wind wing.	Undamaged wind wing.

5. Any of the following situations should alert the officer to the possible need for further investigation.

   Do the driver and the occupants of the vehicle fit that particular vehicle?

Are unclean youths in possession of a large, new, expensive vehicle?

Is an older person driving a kid's hot rod?

Does the vehicle fit in with the neighborhood?

Is the driver familiar with the vehicle?

Is the vehicle being operated smoothly?

Is a vehicle being towed or pushed at an unusually late hour?

Is one vehicle being followed closely by another?

Tow trucks cruising the streets should be checked.

Does the driver attempt to evade arrest for a minor violation?

Does the driver turn onto another street upon seeing a police vehicle and does he fail to pass when he approaches the police vehicle from the rear?

Be suspicious of the driver who rushes back to the police vehicle after the stop has been made. He may not want the officer to look inside the vehicle.

Is the driver nervous?

Does the driver give evasive answers to routine questions by the officer?

Is the driver from another state, or distant city, and is he without luggage?

6. License plates, number required.
   Are the required number of license plates displayed on the vehicle?
   Is the vehicle without any license plates?
   Are passenger vehicle plates on passenger ve-

hicles and commercial vehicle plates on commercial vehicles?

Compare the license number on the registration certificate with the number of the license plate displayed. The vehicle identification number on the certificate should also be compared. No license plates displayed may be an indication the vehicle was just stolen and that the thief removed the license plates so he would not be detected, and is in the process of trying to obtain another set for the vehicle in his possession. However, this may also be a case where the owner is registering the vehicle for the first time in the state and the motor vehicle department has not yet issued license plates for the vehicle. The owner should have in his possession a receipt indicating that the registration fees for the vehicle have been paid, and the receipt should identify the vehicle. This could apply to both new and used vehicles.

If the vehicle is a new vehicle just purchased from a dealer or a used vehicle, with or without license plates on the used vehicle, the dealer must issue a Dealer's Report Of Sale for the vehicle. A copy of the Dealer's Report Of Sale must be affixed to the windshield and a temporary paper plate affixed to the rear of the vehicle. There is a Dealer's Report Of Sale form for NEW vehicles and one for USED vehicles. Each are clearly marked. (See Illus 14 and Illus. 15.) Note that each has an imprinted number on it; upper right for new vehicles and upper left for used. This number MUST correspond with the number on the temporary paper plate.

STATE OF CALIFORNIA

19 66   **NEW**   N⁰ 285026

DEPT. OF MOTOR VEHICLES

NOTICE TO OTHER STATES
This is a notice of purchase of vehicle. Do not use as an application for registration and/or title.

AUTOMOBILE	COMMERCIAL	TRAILER	MOTORCYCLE

IMPORTANT! Do Not Fail to Check Vehicle Type Above

Sold to:
(Print true full name)_____
LAST   FIRST   MIDDLE

Address_____

City_____ County_____

Make_____ Vehicle
Identification No._____

Date sold_____ Body Type_____ Model_____
NAME OR NUMBER

Legal owner:
(Print true full name)_____

Address_____

Dealer's Name_____ Dealer's No._____

Address_____

City_____

REG. 397 (REV. 6-65) 49861-900 7-65 1,650M DUP ① ◇ F [30]   IMPORTANT ☞ [OVER]

1966—STATE OF CALIFORNIA—1966
DEPARTMENT OF MOTOR VEHICLES DEALER'S REPORT OF SALE (Paper Plate Copy)

0285026

INSTRUCTIONS—Display on rear of new vehicle. When so displayed, with copy of Report of Sale on windshield, vehicle may be operated until evidence of registration is received, provided the original copy of Dealer's Report of Sale and Fees are submitted to Department of Motor Vehicles within TEN days of date of delivery of vehicle.

Illus. 14.

Dealer's Report of Sale—new vehicle. Courtesy California Department of Motor Vehicles.

N⁰ 5460127

DEALER NOTICE

Before delivery to purchaser this part of the report of sale shall be affixed to vehicle It describes

USED VEHICLE 1966

Resident County of _____

Residence or
Business address _____

Name of Purchaser _____
(Print true full name)   FIRST   MIDDLE   LAST

City _____ County _____

Make of
Vehicle _____ Vehicle
Identification No. _____

Body Type _____   Year Model _____   Last Registered State of: _____
SEDAN, BUS, TRUCK, TANK, ETC.

Last Registered With
in 19 _____ License No. _____   Validation No. _____

Do Vehicle Identification
Numbers on Ownership
Certificate and vehicle correspond? _____
YES OR NO

Dealer's Name _____ By _____
SIGNATURE OF AUTHORIZED AGENT

Address _____

City _____

Dealer's No. _____ Date Sold _____

1966 ORIGINAL

Signature of Purchaser _____

REG. 51 (REV. 6-65)   49851-900 7-65 2,150M DUP ① [20] OSP

1966—STATE OF CALIFORNIA—1966
DEPARTMENT OF MOTOR VEHICLES DEALER'S REPORT OF SALE (Paper Plate Copy)

5460127

INSTRUCTIONS—Display on rear of vehicle. When so displayed, with copy of Report of Sale on windshield, vehicle may be operated until evidence of registration is received, provided the original copy of Dealer's Report of Sale and Fees are submitted to Department of Motor Vehicles within TWENTY days of date of delivery of vehicle.

Illus. 15.
Dealer's Report of Sale—used vehicle. Courtesy of California Department of Motor Vehicles.

7. Mounting of license plates.

Are the license plates mounted in plain view?

Are the license plates securely fastened?

Are the license plates wired on or loose?

Is one license plate mounted on top of another?

Do both front and rear license plates bear the same numbers?

Inspection of the bolts holding the license plates in place may indicate recent removal. Attention should be directed to the area of the holes on the face of the license plate where the bolts hold the plate in place. Look for finger marks on the plate, signs of a tool having been used on the bolt, and indications that the bolt threads have been cleaned by running the nut over them. Some rear license plates are so mounted that the rear bumper or a trailer hitch ball obscures them.

8. Dented license plates on the rear of the vehicle. Most rear license plate mountings, especially those on the trunk lid, are not situated so that damage to the license plate is likely to result. Where a license plate is found in this area and it is damaged, chances are good that it came from the front of another vehicle. Front license plates are usually mounted on the front bumper in a location where they are easily damaged. Nicks, scratches, bugs, and road tar are signs suggesting that the license plate came from the front of a vehicle.

9. Rear license plate light not operative. License plate light not operative during darkness when other lights are functioning may be a clue the thief did not have another license plate to sub-

stitute for the one on the stolen vehicle and may have cut the wire or broken the light bulb. On the other hand, the license plate may be from another vehicle and the light made inoperative so the plate cannot be seen. The possibility of another crime having been committed or about to be committed should not be overlooked.

10. Clean auto - dirty license plate.
Clean license plate - dirty auto.
This may be a clue that license plates have been installed from another vehicle. Extra dirty plates may be an indication the driver wants to conceal the numerals. When examining these license plates, particular attention should be directed to the bolts and the areas around the bolts for finger marks in the dirt. Motor vehicle departments issue only new license plates to new vehicles, although older vehicles are issued new plates if the old plates are lost.

11. License plate number series.
Do the license plate numerals correspond with the series of license plates issued with respect to the age of the vehicle?

Example: Old series plates or original series plates on a new vehicle; AAA 111 license numbers issued in 1963 may not belong on a 1970 model vehicle when other 1970 models are being issued ZZZ 123.

And in states such as California that issued a metal license place in 1963 and validation stickers for that license plate for subsequent years, a 1969 model vehicle could have an old series plate if the plates were issued by a motor vehicle office in a small county where there are very few vehicles. However, the license plates should not display any validation sticker other than for the year it was issued and thereafter.

Example: A 1969 model vehicle purchased in July 1969 may have been issued series license plates with number AAA 999, but the only validation stickers it should have would be for 1969 and subsequent years.

12. Have license figures been altered?

Have the number or letters on the license plates been painted over or has tape been used to alter their appearance? Two license plates can be cut in half, and each half used to make a new plate. This is a sign a professional operator is at work rather than the "every day-type" auto thief.

13. Ignition.

Is there a key in the ignition switch?

Does the driver fail to turn off the engine?

Will the key operate the ignition switch?

Is the key a decoy?

Illus. 16
Exposed wires hanging from under the dash.

Illus. 17
This illustrates the ease with which a new switch may be substituted for the old.

Has the ignition switch been been removed? Are wires exposed or hanging from under the dashboard? (see Illus. 16)

If there is no key in the ignition switch and there are no wires hanging from under the dashboard, examine the back of the switch for tin foil or a ball of steel wool. Both make good "jumpers" with little effort required to place them in use. Most ignition switches in late model vehicles are so designed that the wire loom is equipped with a female type receptacle into which the switch plugs. (Illus. 17) An ignition switch with the keys can be purchased from a dealer for the make of vehicle to be stolen. The thief enters the vehicle, unplugs the wires from the vehicle's ignition switch, leaving that switch in place, and with a dummy key in it to give the appearance it is in operation, plugs in the switch he purchased, starts the vehicle and drives away. In addition, inspection should be made under the hood in the engine compartment. Attention should be directed to the ignition coil and the battery for wires leading from one to the other for "hot wiring." Inspection should be made of the materials of both the battery and the coil for signs an alligator type clip has been used. These signs will usually be light scratches.

14. Certificates of ownership.
Registration certificates. (See Illus. 18-23)
Bill of sale.
Automobile Dealer's Report of Sale. (See Illus. 14, 15)

CASHIER'S TEMPORARY RECEIPT

STATE OF CALIFORNIA
DEPARTMENT OF MOTOR VEHICLES

R 571933 -T

0A 46 169170

LAST LICENSE NO.   VEHICLE I.D. No.

USE TAX

$ MAKE $ 64

CASH
CHECK
M.O.
BAR

$

REFUND ORDER NO.

R Chelimidrs

REGISTERED OWNER'S NAME

PLATE   **375 ATB**

ADDRESS

STICKER   **C5199440**

CITY   CALIF.   ZIP CODE

7011

OFFICE NO.   DATE   CASHIER'S NO.

Alterations or erasures will void this form. Read instructions on reverse side.

ADM 340 (REV. 8-69)   35016-900 8-69 3,000M ④T OSP

Illus. 18.

Receipt issued by Department of Motor Vehicles to new owner showing registration application had been made and fees paid. NOTE that sticker number on this form and tab number on Illus. 19 are the same.

Does the vehicle described on the registration document correspond with the vehicle being checked?

Does the license plate number and the vehicle identification number on the registration certificate or bill of sale correspond with those of the vehicle?

Is part of the registration certificate or other document destroyed so that the portion which contains the license number or the vehicle identification number is missing?

Is the registration certificate for the current year?

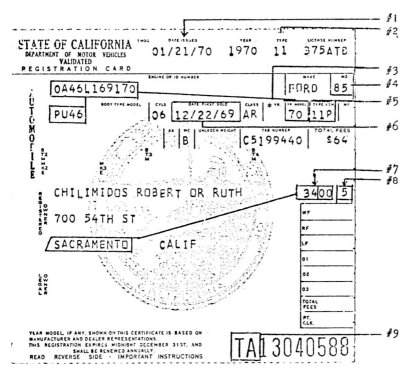

Illus. 19

This registration certificate is issued following application. This form is attached to the "pink slip" and prepared on data processing machines. Size - 4¼" x 4½". NOTE that all typing is on a straight line and even and that the edges are perforated. The document number, TA13040588, will also appear on the "pink slip".

(1) DATE OF ISSUE.
This is the date the Department of Motor Vehicles issued the title to this vehicle.

(2) TYPES OF CERTIFICATES ISSUED.

	VEHICLE REGISTRATIONS		
TYPE OF VEHICLE	NEW	RENEWAL	NON RESIDENT
AUTOMOBILE	11	12	13
MOTOR CYCLE	21	22	23
COMMERCIAL	31	32	33
TRAILER	41	42	43
ELECTRIC AUTOMOBILE	14	15	16
ELECTRIC MOTORCYCLE	24	25	26
ELECTRIC COMMERCIAL	34	35	36

(3) The year model of the vehicle, the vehicle identification number and the body type model must correspond.

(4) MONTH CODE.
Sequential numerical designation of the month the certificate was issued beginning with number 1 on January 1963. January 1970, therefore is the 85th month. February 1970 was the 86th month and so on.

(5) VEHICLE TYPE CODE.
The numerical designation is a repeat of #2. The letter code is as follows:

A. Ambulance
B. Bus
C. Camp trailer
D. Dump
E. Panel delivery
F. Flatbed
G. Tractor
H. Chassis
K. Tank
L. Log bunk
M. Military
N. Transit mix

O. All passenger vehicles and motorcycles
P. Pickup
Q. Private owned school bus
R. Refrigerator
S. Station wagon
T. Trailer coach or house
V. Van
W. Transport
X. Taxi or limousine for hire
Y. Miscellaneous
Z. Special construction equipment

(6) DATE FIRST SOLD.
This is the date the dealer first sold the vehicle.

(7) COUNTY CODE.
There are four digits for the county codes. The first two digits represent the county of residence code (34) and the last two digits represent the county of employment code (00). Where the county of employment differs than that of the residence, that code number will be indicated. Where the county of residence and employment are the same, the last two digits will be 00.

Example: Code 3457 - Owner lives in Sacramento County (34) and is employed in Yolo County (57).

NOTE: The code for the residence must correspond with the county in which the city, as indicated on the certificate ,is located.

Also refer to county code numbers.

CALIFORNIA COUNTY CODE NUMBERS.

Alameda	01	Marin	21	San Luis Obispo	40
Alpine	02	Mariposa	22	San Mateo	41
Amador	03	Mendocino	23	Santa Barbara	42
Butte	04	Merced	24	Santa Clara	43
Calaveras	05	Modoc	25	Santa Cruz	44
Colusa	06	Mono	26	Shasta	45
Contra Costa	07	Monterey	27	Sierra	46
Del Morte	08	Napa	28	Siskiyou	47
El Dorado	09	Nevada	29	Solano	48
Fresno	10	Orange	30	Sonoma	49
Glenn	11	Placer	31	Stanislaus	50
Humboldt	12	Plumas	32	Sutter	51
Imperial	13	Riverside	33	Tehama	52
Inyo	14	Sacramento	34	Trinity	53
Kern	15	San Benito	35	Tulare	54
Kings	16	San Bernardino	36	Tuolumne	55
Lake	17	San Diego	37	Ventura	56
Lassen	18	San Francisco	38	Yolo	57
Los Angeles	19	San Joaquin	39	Yuba	58
Madera	20				

(8) TYPE OF OWNERSHIP.
  1. No legal owner - none required.
  2. Legal owner on transfer.
  3. No legal owner on transfer.
  4. Legal ownership issued.
  5. No legal ownership issued.
  6. Legal owner - records only.
  7. No legal owner - records only.
  8. Legal owner - registration card issued.
  9. No legal owner - registration card only.
  There is a legal owner on even numbered codes, sole ownership on odd code numbers.

(9) SERIAL NUMBER PREFIXES ON REGISTRATION CERTIFI-CATES.

TA	Title Automobile
TC	Title Commercial
TM	Title Motorcycle
TT	Title Trailer
TTA	Special Typed Automobile
TTC	Special Typed Commercial
TTM	Special Typed Motorcycle
TTT	Special Typed Trailer
VA	Validated Automobile Registration Card Only
VC	Validated Commercial Registration Card Only
VM	Validated Motorcycle Registration Card Only
VT	Validated Trailer Registration Card Only
TVA	Special Typed Validated Automobile
TVC	Special Typed Validated Commercial
TVM	Special Typed Validated Motorcycle
TVT	Special Typed Validated Trailer
GA	Goldenrod Automobile
GC	Goldenrod Commercial
GM	Goldenrod Motorcycle
GT	Goldenrod Trailer
TGA	Special Typed Goldenrod Automobile
TGC	Special Typed Goldenrod Commercial
TGM	Special Typed Goldenrod Motorcycle
TGT	Special Typed Goldenrod Trailer
QC	Quarterly Commercial
QT	Quarterly Trailer
QGC	Quarterly Goldenrod Commercial
QGT	Quarterly Goldenrod Trailer
TQGC	Special Typed Goldenrod Commercial
TQGT	Special Typed Goldenrod Trailer
TQC	Special Typed Quarterly Commercial
TQT	Special Typed Quarterly Trailer

Does the registration certificate, bill of sale, or dealer's report of sale appear to have been altered or forged?

If there is no registration certificate, why not? Did the state which issued the registration certificate also issue the license plates?

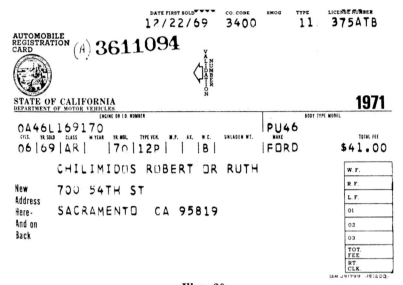

Illus. 20

This registration certificate is issued for renewal. When validated it will be stamped with the current year tab number, (A) above, by a hand stamp. Size - 3¼″ x 4¾″. NOTE that all typing is on a straight line and even and the edges are perforated.

Is the name of the driver the same as that indicated as the owner on the registration certificate?

If the driver of the vehicle is unable to provide proof of ownership or proof of having proper possession, it may be advisable to have the radio dispatcher contact the owner by telephone for verification while the person in possession is detained.

15. Examination of the vehicle identification number. (Also refer to chapter 11.)

Does the vehicle identification number plate or do the numbers on the plate appear to have been tampered with or altered?

Are screws holding the identification number

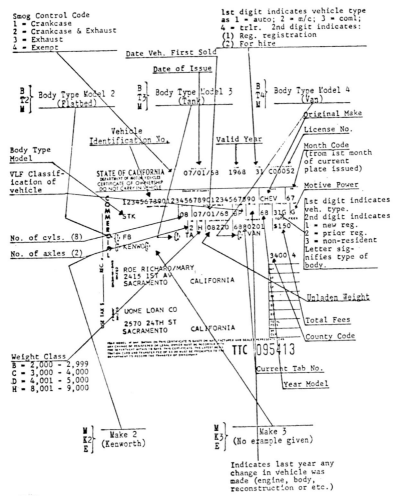

Ill.
Registration certificate of a commercial vehicle
showing explinations for the various codes.

Illus. 21

Registration certificate of a commercial vehicle showing explanations
for the various codes.

plate in place instead of the spot welds or
rivets used by the manufacturer?

Will a little pull from under the vehicle identification plate "pop" it off indicating that it

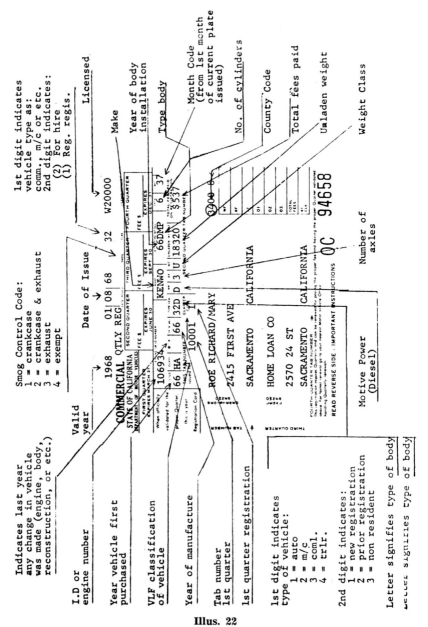

Illus. 22

Registration certificate issued on a quarterly basis showing explanations for the various codes.

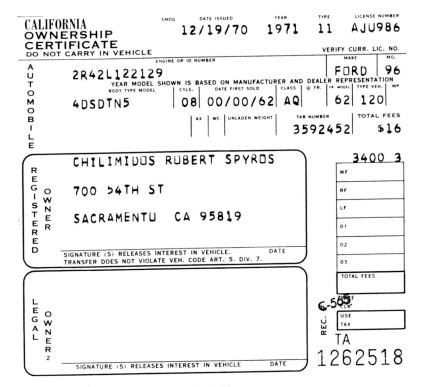

| CALIFORNIA OWNERSHIP CERTIFICATE | SMOG | DATE ISSUED 12/19/70 | YEAR 1971 | TYPE 11 | LICENSE NUMBER AJU986 |

Illus. 23.

This ownership document, also referred to as the "pink slip", has been revised and issued starting late in 1970. Note that signatures required to relinquish ownership are now shown on the face - not on the back side as before.

is being held in place with chewing gum, tar or glue?

Has the identification number been ground off, destroyed with a chisel or punch, or peened with a hammer so that the numbers are illegible?

Is the vehicle identification number plate missing?

Perhaps that part of the vehicle upon which the vehicle identification number plate should be attached has been damaged in an accident and replaced with a new part. The new part will not have an identification number or plate. Perhaps the replacement part has been obtained from another wrecked vehicle and now displays the wrecked vehicle's identification number.

Has the engine number been ground off?

Keep in mind when examining engines and transmissions for identification numbers: Identification numbers are STAMPED INWARD, usually on a smooth pad, and RAISED numbers indicate a casting, forging, firing sequence, or parts number. When doubt or uncertainty arises in the officer's mind regarding vehicle identification numbers or plates, it may be advisable to summon the assistance of the auto theft specialist who is familiar with vehicle identification numbers.

8

IDENTIFICATION OF PERSONS

The Identity of Victim, Witness and Suspect.

Identification is the key to every successful investigation. Therefore the certainty and completeness of the identification of the victim, suspect or witness should be the primary goal of every investigation. Insofar as it is available, the minimum information gathered should indicate to the officer who he is looking for and where he may be found. Lacking this basic information can lead to dismissal of charges against the suspect by the court because a victim or witness was unavailable to testify against the accused.

The good investigator will follow a procedure in obtaining information relating to the identification of persons that seldoms varies in its pattern. Following a standard form of procedure is important for it readily becomes an automatic action or habit which cannot be easily shaken in moments of stress or when working under pressure. George Payton, in his book, Patrol Procedure suggests a mnemonic code that may help in establishing a standard form of procedure.

1. N-S-R-A (name, sex, race, age)
   or Numb Skulls Rarely Agree

2. H-W-H-E-C-P-C-J (height, weight, hair, eyes, complexion, physical marks, clothing, jewelry)

or Have We Had Escaping Criminals Pulling Cunning Jobs

In following such a step by step procedure it will be necessary to interview many persons, some of whom will be helpful to the case while others may not, but there is no short cut or substitute for persistence and hard work. During the investigation it is well to remember that it is often just as important to be able to go back at a later date to a person who supplied you with the information as it is to be able to use the information in a court of law and this is where correctness and the completeness of the investigative report pays off.

Procedural Check List for Identification.

Employment of the following check list will insure your including the important elements of identification of persons in your report.

1. **Name:** This may be written in the report in the following manner:

    Witness: John Peter ADAMS (WMA 34)
             1234 Center Street, City - Empire 33123

    List the first, middle and last name. **Capitalize** the last or surname for easy reference. Include nicknames and/or aliases.

    It is always good practice to ask the person being interviewed if the name he has given is his true name. Ask him to spell it even though it may be a common name. Do not take the spelling of any name for granted. A misspelled name can cause doubt as to the proper identification of an individual. It is very important to obtain the **complete name** correctly.

Example: Allen, Allan, Allyn
Carl, Karl
Earle, Earle
John, Jahn, Jon
Smith, Smyth, Smithe

Many persons are referred to by an abbreviation of their first name, by initials, a nickname, or by their middle name.

Example: A. B. Adams, A. Bruce Adams,
Al for Albert, Alexander or Alvin
Bill for William, Wilbert, Wilburn
Betty for Elizabeth
Bobbie for Roberta or Barbara
Bud, Buddy, Butch or Chuck for
Charles or Clarence
Jack for John

Many first names are also commonly used as last names.

Example: George Peter THOMAS
Thomas Peter GEORGE

In other cases first names and last names because of their foreign origin sound strange and unusual and can be confusing as one tries to determine what the last name is.

Example: Spyros Nicholas POLOUS
Tsuando Quong YOKOYAMA

First names of married women should be their own given name, never their husband's first name. When possible also include their maiden name.

> Example: (Mrs.) Thelma Mae GEORGE
> (maiden name TAYLOR)
>
> **Do not** record as Mrs. Thomas P. GEORGE

In cases involving juveniles, both parent's names (mother and father) should be recorded. Particular attention should be given to the child who lives with foster parents, or whose parents have remarried and the last name of the parent and the child differ.

2. **Sex:** The name alone does not always single out man from woman. To the person who actually saw an individual, sex should be distinguishable. However, there are some names commonly used by both sexes that do not distinguish one from the other.

> Example:
> > Bobbie - Bobby
> > Evelyn, Leslie, Marion, Shirley, Vivian
> > Francis - Frances
> > Gene - Jean
> > Tony, Toni

3. **Race:** The designation of race is for one purpose only and that is to assist the law enforcement officer in identifying persons as victims, witnesses and suspects. It is not intended to single out any race or ethnic group and attempt to thus place them in an adverse light. The color of a

man's skin is a primary distinguishing characteristic for purposes of description of the appearance of an individual. Names alone cannot identify individuals, especially when the same name
may be common to more than one race. Aside
from the color of the skin race origin is sometimes apparent through traditional dress or ac-
cent of speech. Racial groups are identified as
black, white, yellow and red.

4. **Age:** First, obtain date and place of birth. For
identification purposes age is often hard to accurately ascertain since it can be influenced by
many factors among which might be the varying
circumstances of life and racial background. A
generalization, by sticking to age groups, such
as teen-ager, middle aged or elderly will probably in most cases suffice.

5. **Height:** Even the best witnesses can be and often
are poor judges of height. Have them make a
comparison with some person present rather than
asking for height in feet and inches.

6. **Weight:** This information is also subject to poor
judgment. Comparison with a person whom the
witness regards as of similar height and build
to the suspect, is often helpful.

7. **Hair:** The description should not just say,
"blond", "black" or "grey". Be specific about
color or peculiarity of color.

   Indicate if it is curly, kinky or straight.

   Is the growth thick or thin? Are there bald
spots? Where?

   Specify style of cut.

8. **Eyes:** Include more than just the color of the eyes. Are they small, deep set, protruding, slanted, etc. Are glasses habitually worn and if so what style frames.

9. **Complexion:** The skin tone, is it dark, fair, ruddy or pale? Are there skin blemishes, birthmarks, scars - what is their location?

10. **Other Marks:** Limps, deformities, bad teeth, amputations, fingerprint classifications, tattoos, speech impediments, appearance of clothing - neat, dirty - a uniform, the type of jewelry or watch that is habitually worn.

11. **Address:** If the investigating officer obtains the full address and records it in his report he may later save many hours that otherwise could have been spent in going over the same ground twice in search of a witness or suspect. This is particularily important when subpeonas and warrants are to be served. Be sure and include the business address (if any) as well as the residence address in your report.

12. **Telephone:** Do not overlook the telephone number. You may save yourself hours of time in running down witnesses by making appointments in advance. When recording business telephones always be sure and include the extension number, if there is one.

9

INTERVIEWS

In proceeding with the interview there are two aspects of the problem that immediately present themselves. Number one, you have the willing contributor, who makes himself readily available for questioning, and number two, you have the unwilling contributor who doesn't want "to become involved" for any number of reasons. How one goes about asking questions to which others will respond depends largely on the interviewer and how he presents himself. It is recognized that not all persons have that quality which makes them successful interviewers, however even the best can and should, from time to time, add a little polish to their technique.

The Victim is Interviewed.

The victim is generally the first person interviewed by the police. After discovering the loss, the victim calls the police. The officer responding must interview him to determine what happened and to establish that a crime actually was committed. An exception to this is when a person is apprehended in a vehicle not yet reported stolen, and careful interviewing by an efficient officer establishes that the vehicle is stolen and the owner is not yet aware of the theft. For the most part however, the victim discovers the loss first.

In most cases he will not be able to furnish the investigating officer much information as to the circumstances surrounding the theft. In other instances he may not want to provide the officer with any information other than that the vehicle is missing. Perhaps he wants to cover up another crime, or that he loaned the vehicle to someone and now wants it back but, since he is unable to get the vehicle himself, he reports it stolen to the police so they can find it for him. The investigating officer must approach each auto theft case with the thought that possibly another crime has been committed, or that the vehicle has been repossessed. The victim must be questioned thoroughly on the first contact as to his whereabouts **prior to, during** and **after** the theft.

"Sizing up" of victim through his knowledge of theft.

Ascertain what knowledge he has concerning the theft. Quiz the victim regarding the equipment on his vehicle and the items in it. Record how the items and the equipment may be identified, where they were purchased, and the amount paid for them. This is particularily pertinent in the event the vehicle is recovered stripped. The officer should encourage the victim to talk about the vehicle, what he likes or dislikes about it, and whether or not the vehicle had given any trouble. Ascertain also if there is a mortgage on the vehicle, the amount of the mortgage and the monthly payments, or if any work has been done on the vehicle or accessories installed for which there is an unpaid balance due. "Size up" the victim. Does it appear he is living far beyond his means and that this theft may be a means of relieving some of the financial pressure? This should be given particular attention when the person reporting the theft is a "hot-rod" enthusiast whose vehicle has been equipped with racing equipment. Some thefts have been fraudulently reported by an owner who stripped his own vehicle to collect from the insurance company. He knows his vehicle will not be recovered, as he has cut it up and disposed of it at an iron mill. Many thousands of dollars have been paid out by insurance companies whose policy holders have falsely reported the theft of their vehicles or items from them.

The victim's statement and supporting statements.

Ascertain if the victim has witnesses who will testify in his behalf and who will support his statements, and what he thinks they will say. It may be best to accept the victim's first statement at its face value. Once the victim has given his story and he feels the officer has accepted it, he may let his guard down and give himself away regarding another crime.

Re-interview where fraud is suspected.

After the vehicle has been recovered the officer may desire to re-interview the victim, depending upon the circumstances under which the vehicle is recovered. For example: the vehicle is recovered burned. Some reasons may be:

1. Financial problems
2. Insurance fraud
3. Domestic problems
4. Dissatisfaction with the vehicle

The owner should be contacted as soon after the recovery as possible and his person examined for odor of smoke or gasoline and general cleanliness.

Re-interview where "hit and run" is suspected.

Example: The vehicle is recovered with extensive damage resulting from a traffic collision. The owner reports the vehicle stolen in an effort to cover up a hit and run. The officer may desire to question those at the accident scene for any information enabling him to identify the responsible vehicle and driver. Some reasons why the suspect left the scene may be:

1. He was intoxicated and did not want to be arrested for drunk driving
2. He has no insurance
3. His driving privileges have been suspended or revoked

The officer should also note at the interview with the person reporting the vehicle stolen whether this person has any sign of injury. After the vehicle is recovered and found to have damage of the type which would result from a traffic collision, the officer may confront the reporting party with these facts and the officer's own observations.

Re-interview when victim is robbery suspect.

Example: If a robbery has been reported, the officer should attempt to match up the description of a person reporting a vehicle stolen, and the vehicle, with the description of the robbery suspect and vehicle used in perpetration of the crime.

Witnesses to Auto Theft.

A witness is a competent person who possesses facts concerning an incident which he obtained himself through personal contact or knowledge.

Witnesses should be located and interviewed as soon as possible. They should be carefully interviewed, particularly those whom the victim indicated would be witnesses for him. It would be well to point out that their names were given by the victim, and an explanation of the conspiracy law should be given to the potential witnesses in the event that circumstances require a false theft report.

Witnesses in auto theft cases are usually difficult to locate. This is primarily due to the fact most vehicles stolen have been left unattended with the keys in the ignition switch. The thief just gets in and drives away. There is nothing spectacular about this, and most potential witnesses do not realize a crime has been committed. Nevertheless, areas where vehicles are stolen should be canvassed in an effort to locate someone with knowledge of the crime. Until this is done, witnesses may not be aware of the crime. The same attention should be given the area where the stolen vehicle is recovered.

When a witness is located and he has information pertaining to the crime being investigated, as much information as possible should be drawn from him. Interviewing a witness requires tact so as not to frighten him away or result in his saying nothing other than "I don't know." This is a very important phase of any investigation. There is no substitute for a willingness to testify and present pertinent information as a competent witness in a court of law. It is not beneficial to anyone if the officer is unable to secure information because of reluctance by a witness to divulge it.

The officer must bear in mind that some people do not like to talk with police officers, perhaps because of a past unpleasant experience. Others do not want to say anything for fear of getting someone in trouble, while others just do not want to be bothered losing time from work to appear in court. How the officer extracts information from a potential witness depends largely upon himself and his approach, the witness's attitude, and the incident. The officer's approach should not be with pen and note book in hand. He should first attempt to win the confidence of the prospective witness. The witness should be allowed to tell his story in his own way and in his own words, without any interruption from the officer. After the witness has finished and the officer has evaluated the statement and feels it contains elements related to the crime which will be of value to the investigation, he should review the statement with the witness and record it.

Evaluation of the witness and his statement.

Evaluate each witness and his statement for its worth to the case. No useful purpose is served in obtaining a witness just for having a witness. Determine if the witness is a relative or a friend of either the victim or the suspect. Disinterested people make the best witnesses; however, friends and relatives should not be overlooked as potentially useful witnesses. Therefore, indicate the relationship of victim to witness, if any. No two people see the same event in exactly the same way. The officer must not stop after obtaining what may appear to be a complete account from one person. After several people have been interviewed and many bits of information obtained the entire picture may change. Keep in mind that the officer's investigation can be made a little easier by those who have information and are willing to share it. Keep an open mind and let facts speak for themselves, making sure the statements give the same picture as do the facts.

Suspects.

Once a suspect has been apprehended, he should be interviewed regarding the crime known to have been committed. This area is rather difficult for the interviewer, for the person has now become a prime suspect, whether in custody or not, and he must be advised of his constitutional rights. The United States Supreme Court has rendered some decisions whereby police officers must respect the constitutional rights of all, including, most of all, those suspected or accused of a crime. In two recent celebrated cases, Escobedo vs. Illinois (1964) and Miranda vs. Arizona (1966), the Supreme Court found that the fourteenth amendment to the United States Constitution had been violated resulting in definite guide lines being issued by the Supreme Court for police officers to abide by, with respect to interviewing suspects. These decisions have caused considerable controversy in the law enforcement field. However, it might well be noted here that both these decisions were handed down by a five to four majority, indicating that although these cases were decided in favor of the defendants, it was by a very slim margin. Perhaps what the court is saying here is that either the police recognize and respect the rights of the people they are entrusted to protect, or the Supreme Court will set free those whose Constitutional rights have been violated by the police regardless of the crime, as punishment to the officer for failing to perform his duties in accordance with the laws of the land.

Advising suspect of his Constitutional rights.

As a matter of policy officers should make it a practice to admonish all those whom they suspect of having committed a crime or those in custody for having committed a crime, of their constitutional rights, which are:

1. That the suspect has the right to remain silent.
2. That anything he says can and will be used against him in court.
3. That he has the right to consult with an attorney and to have an attorney present with him during the interview by the police.
4. That if he can not afford an attorney himself, one will be appointed to represent him before questioning.

Following the admonition, the suspect must express his understanding of his rights and state he is willing and capable of voluntarily, knowingly and intelligently waiving his rights before discussing the matter with the police.

Procedure after admonition as to rights.

Once the admonition is out of the way, the officer may either continue his interview, or stop the questioning if the person elects not to say anything.

If the officer is able to continue, he should "firm up" the crime he is investigating and then attempt to clear up other crimes that the suspect may be responsible for.

Search of suspects person and property.

A search of his person and property should be made, and the items found should be carefully examined for their worth as evidence or leads to other crimes. Some items of value as evidence may be;

Vehicle keys.

Vehicle registration certificates or related documents.

All types of credit cards.

Gasoline charge receipts.

Another person's identification documents.

House or business establishment keys.

Amount and denomination of money in suspects possession.

Pawn shop receipts.

Items out of harmony with suspect's circumstances (such as jewlery, rare coins, typewriter, check protector machine, etc.).

Interview Following A Vehicle Stop.

Once the vehicle has been stopped (vehicle stops are discussed in chapter 10) the officer will want to talk with the occupants of the vehicle in an effort to determine whether they have proper possession of the vehicle. The driver should be requested to alight from the vehicle and to bring the keys with him. Ask him such questions as:

What do ALL the keys belong to?

Who owns the vehicle?

Who is the registered owner of the vehicle?

Who is the legal owner of the vehicle?

How much gasoline is registered on the gauge?

What is the speedometer mileage reading?

What contents are in the trunk?

What contents are in the glove compartment?

(With the suspect looking away from the vehicle) Does the vehicle have whitewall or blackwall tires?

How long has he owned the vehicle?

Where was the vehicle purchased?

Where is vehicle serviced? (check lube record stickers on door)

It may be necessary for the officer to have his radio dispatcher call the owner of record and ascertain from him who should have possession of the vehicle.

At this point the officer may have some reason to suspect the vehicle is stolen, but he is not sure. He may proceed with questioning in an exploratory manner in an effort to determine a fact. The driver need not be admonished of his constitutional rights. However, when the inquiry advances to a point where the officer should have reasonable cause to believe a crime has been committed, the admonishment MUST be given.

10

RECOVERING THE STOLEN VEHICLE

Recovering The Stolen Vehicle

Efficient recovery of stolen property and it's return to the rightful owner creates public confidence in the police. As soon as a vehicle is reported stolen, the police should make every effort to locate the vehicle, apprehend the thieves, and return the vehicle to it's owner.

Illus. 24.
An abandoned vehicle.

Few vehicles are recovered while occupied; most are recovered abandoned — some stripped or wrecked, others intact. Some are left parked on busy roadways where the traffic flow is heavy and constant, while others are parked in the parking lots of super markets or apartment complexes or at airline terminals. Others are abandoned in country wooded areas, and some are pushed into rivers or lakes. (Illus. 24) Stolen vehicles may also be found in garages of unoccupied homes in residential areas, commercial garages, or in front of police stations.

In many cases alert officers locate vehicles under suspicious circumstances on which there is no report of theft in the file. A telephone call to the owner reveals that the vehicle has been stolen without the owners awareness of the loss.

Areas of surveillance for stolen vehicles.

Areas that should be kept under surveillance while on patrol:
  1. Public parking areas of shopping centers
  2. Parking areas of motels and hotels
  3. Parking areas of apartment complexes
  4. School parking areas
  5. Drag strips
  6. Homes of hot-rodders
  7. Places where vehicles are being worked on during late or unusual hours
  8. All "back yard" type auto dismantling operations
  9. Tow trucks or trucks with booms on the streets during late or unusual hours

Officers should develop contacts with:
1. Wrecking yards
2. School auto shops
3. Commercial auto repair shops and parts stores
4. Shops and garages that cater to the speed or hot-rod enthusiasts
5. New and used automobile dealers
6. Iron salvage or junk yards

Examination of the Recovered Vehicle

The most important single phase of any criminal investigation is the collection, identification, and preservation of the evidence. Just as much care must be exercised in the examination of the stolen vehicle upon its recovery, and to the area where it was parked, as in the examination of the scene of any other crime. **This is the crime scene.** Protect it and examine it thoroughly. Look and you may find—don't look and you won't know what "you're missin". As we attempt to seek answers to the **what, why, when, where, who,** and **how** questions from the victim, we again attempt to find the answers to these same questions at the recovery scene. Be meticulous in your investigation. Follow through on a standard investigative procedure that will minimize the possibility of error or omission.

Steps in examination of recovery scene.

Examination of the recovery scene should be completed in steps to insure the best possible results as suggested here:

1. Examine identification numbers and letters to avoid errors. Do not write a 5 so that it may be mistaken for an S, a 2 for a Z, etc.

2. Do not rush up to an abandoned stolen vehicle. Park the police vehicle away from the stolen vehicle and carefully approach it. A quick glance into the interior will reveal if anyone is laying down in the vehicle. Feel the hood of the stolen vehicle. If it is warm, a stake out may be warranted on the possibility that someone may return to it. A stake out may also be considered when the vehicle is parked in a shopping center or school yard. If the stolen vehicle is abandoned on a freeway which is fenced for limited access, suspects may be on foot, hitch-hiking. A check for pedestrians in the vicinity of the stolen vehicle should be made. If there is a heavy film of dust or dirt on the upper portion of the body and glass, and there is debris around the tires, chances are the vehicle has been standing for quite some time.

3. Examine the immediate area where the vehicle is parked for signs of:

Tire marks

Footprints

Any piece of paper, cloth, or tool which may be connected to a person or a metal object, like an empty can, from which fingerprints may be obtained.

4. The exterior of the vehicle should be examined.

Signs of traffic collision damage on the exterior body which may be connected to a hit-run.

Broken glass or other signs of forced entry.

Missing or altered license plates.

Missing parts, such as, engine, transmission, wheels and tires, etc.

Signs of latent prints.

Illus. 25
Dusting exterior for prints.

Illus. 26
Ignition switch "hot wired" or removed.

5. The exterior of the vehicle should be dusted for prints prior to the examination of the interior (Illus. 25).

6. Examination of the interior.

Ignition switch — removed or hot wired (Illus. 26).

Vehicle identification number plate—tampered with or missing.

Registration certificate.

Missing parts — bucket seats, upholstery, or dash instruments.

Examine behind the dashboard.

In glove compartment.

In ash trays.

Under the seats.

Under the floor mats.

Above the sun visors.

Any clothing in the vehicle.

Any boxes or suitcases.

Look for latent prints.

7. Examine under the hood.
   Ignition system—hot wired.
   Missing parts

8. Examine the trunk compartment.

9. Examine the under carriage.

10. Examine the area where the vehicle was re-covered for several blocks.

Location and preservation of evidence.

When evidence has been located the proper steps must be taken for its preservation. Latent prints, paints chips, gasoline purchase receipts, and missing parts from damaged areas may be useful for comparison or identification should a suspect be developed.

This procedure should be employed especially in cases where the stolen vehicle is stripped. Careful inspection of the vehicle could also reveal evidence that another crime has been committed.

Examination of the vehicle will reveal the vehicle's general apparent condition and will yield certain bits of evidence. In most cases evidence is present. It is up to the officer to locate it. Record what evidence is located, who located it, and where it was located. Also record what parts or items are apparently missing, such as the tires, engine, transmission, radio, etc. List all the items found in the vehicle. Examine body and fender damage for possible connection with a hit-run accident. The direction the vehicle is parked upon recovery should be noted, as this is a good indication that if any crime has been committed other than the taking of the vehicle, it has been committed somewhere in the direction from which the vehicle came.

Connecting the suspect with the stolen vehicle.

It is virtually impossible to connect a suspect with the theft of a vehicle once the suspect has left the vehicle unless there is some physical evidence, or a witness to the taking or using of the vehicle by the suspect. Therefore, any evidence that would place the suspect in the vehicle is important; even though it in itself is not proof that the vehicle was stolen by the suspect. There is however, a better possibility that the suspect will confess to the crime if confronted with good evidence.

If the ignition system is not hot wired and no key is found in the abandoned stolen vehicle, it is possible the thief may have absent-mindedly taken the key with him when he abandoned the vehicle. Suspects should be searched for any item which may belong to the stolen vehicle such as the registration certificate, gasoline purchase receipts from credit card sales, and keys.

Recovered Vehicle Report

As in the theft report, the recovery report should include as much information as possible to answer the **what, where, when, who, why,** and **how** questions. Again, care must be exercised in preparing the report. Letters and numerals mistaken for something other than what they were intended will result in improper filing and failure to cancel a stolen vehicle report. (Illus. 27, 28, 29, 30).

DEPARTMENT OF CALIFORNIA HIGHWAY PATROL				

VEHICLE REPORT   TYPE (CHECK ONE) ☐ IMPOUNDED ☐ RECOVERED ☐ STORED ☐ RELEASED   *Use Reverse Side for Stolen or Embezzled Vehicles.*

REPORTING DEPT.	AREA/DIVISION	DATE	FILE NO.

DESCRIPTION OF VEHICLE

YEAR	MAKE	BODY TYPE	LICENSE NO. (S)		YEAR	STATE	COLOR (COMBINATION)
			F				
			B				

VEHICLE (IDENTIFICATION NO. (VIN)	VIN CHECK WITH REG ☐ YES ☐ NO	VIN APPEAR ALTERED ☐ YES ☐ NO	ENGINE NO.	SPEEDOMETER READING

REGISTERED OWNER	ADDRESS	PHONE
LEGAL OWNER	ADDRESS	PHONE
DRIVER OR LAST PERSON IN POSSESSION	ADDRESS	PHONE

CIRCUMSTANCES

NAME OF GARAGE	ADDRESS	PHONE

REQUIRED NOTICES SENT TO REGISTERED AND LEGAL OWNERS AND GARAGE (SEC. 22852 VC) ☐ YES ☐ NO	IF NO IS CHECKED, INDICATE REASONS

TOWED FROM (LOC.)	TIME AND DATE TOWED

PERSON REPORTING OCCURRENCE	ADDRESS	PHONE	TIME AND DATE REPORTED

CONDITION OF VEHICLE	DRIVEABLE ☐ YES ☐ NO	WRECKED ☐ YES ☐ NO	STRIPPED ☐ YES ☐ NO

VEH. RETURNED TO OWNER	IF STOLEN, NAME OF REPORTING AGENCY	TELETYPE NO. (RECOVERY)	DATE OF TELETYPE

REMARKS (IF ARREST IS MADE, GIVE FULL NAMES, CHARGES, WHERE BOOKED)

VEHICLE INVENTORY

	YES	NO		YES	NO		CONDITION	LIST PROPERTY TOOLS OTHER ITEMS
CUSHION (FRONT)			SPOTLIGHT(S)			L F. TIRE		
CUSHION (REAR)			FOGLIGHT(S)			R F. TIRE		
REAR VIEW MIRROR			BUMPER (FRONT)			R R. TIRE		
SIDE VIEW MIRROR			BUMPER (REAR)			L R. TIRE		
CIGAR LIGHTER			MOTOR			SPARE TIRE		
RADIO			BATTERY			WHEELS		
CLOCK			AIR CONDITIONER			FENDERS		
HEATER			HUB CAPS			BODY HOOD		
KEYS			FENDER PANTS			TOP		
REGISTRATION			TRANSMISSION			GRILL		
WINDSHIELD WIPER			JACK			UPHOLSTERY		

OFFICER ORDERING VEH. STORED (SIGNATURE) X	I.D. NO.	GARAGE PRINCIPAL OR AGENT STORING VEH. (SIGNATURE) X		TIME AND DATE
APPRAISING OFFICER'S SIGNATURE (SEC. 22704 VC)	I.D. NO.	APPRAISED VALUE		TIME AND DATE OF APPRAISAL

IMPOUND RELEASE NOTIFICATION

TO	ADDRESS	DATE
RELEASE VEHICLE TO	ADDRESS	

SIGNATURE OF CLERK OR OFFICER RELEASING	CERTIFICATION: I, the undersigned, do hereby certify that I am legally authorized and entitled to take possession of above described vehicle.
	SIGNATURE OF OWNER OR LEGAL OWNER OR AGENT OF OWNER

NOTE: *This form is furnished by the Highway Patrol to all peace officers. When completed, mail immediately to: California Highway Patrol, P.O. Box 898, Sacramento, California.*

CHP FORM 180 (REV. 11-67)   PAGE 1 OF 2 PAGES

Illus. 27.
Recovery Report, Caifornia Highway Patrol.

P D Form 86A 3 67

Report No._____

Police Department, City of Sacramento

REPORT OF MOTOR VEHICLE - STOLEN ☒ **RECOVERED** ☐ **IMPOUNDED** ☐ **STORED** ☐

Complainant/Owner_____
Address_____ Phone_____
Business Address_____ Business Phone _____
When stolen/recovered/impounded, Date_____ Hour _____
Where stolen/recovered/impounded_____
Reported by_____ Address _____ Phone_____
Reported to: Officer_____ Date _____ Hour _____

Description of Vehicle:

Make_____ VIN No._____ Mtr. No._____
Type_____ Year Model _____ Color _____ No. Cylinders_____
License No._____ Year _____ State _____
Registered Owner_____ Address _____
Legal Owner_____ Address _____
Condition of vehicle when recovered/impounded/ (Good, stripped, etc.)_____
Out of gas, keys missing, etc._____ Okeh to release _____
Disposition of vehicle (Garage, to owner, etc.)_____

If Vehicle Impounded or Stored-Reason:

Reported stolen_____ Traffic collision_____ Traffic hazard _____ Abandoned_____ Evidence_____ Other_____
Person arrested/cited: Name _____ Charge _____

If Vehicle Stolen:

Locks in use: Ignition_____ Doors_____ Insured With_____
Broadcast_____ Cancelled _____
Auto Status Sent _____ Cancelled _____
Warrant vs._____ Charge _____ Date_____
Connect-ups: Report Nos._____

CLEARANCE:

Person Arrested _____   1   _____
Cleared (Indicate how)_____   _____
Cleared by (Name and Star No.)_____ Div/Detail _____ Date_____

Vehicle Recovered:

Where recovered_____ Date _____
Reported stolen from_____ Date_____ Report No._____
Recovery by (Name and Star No.)_____ Div/Detail _____ Date_____

DETAILS (If stolen vehicle, state size, make and serial number of tires, list accessories, description and value of property in vehicle etc.)

Release and Waiver:

Know all men by these presents. That I _____

of the City of_____ County of_____
State of California, do by these presents, for myself, my heirs, administrators or assigns, release each, every and all duly appointed Peace Officers of any city, county or city and county of the State of California, or of the California Highway Patrol of the State of California, from any claim, action, demands, dues, sums of money, controversies, trespasses, judgments, executions, claims and demands whatsoever, in law or in equity, I ever had or now have or which I, or my heirs, executors, administrators or assigns, hereafter can, shall or may have against any Peace Officer or Peace Officer for, upon or by reason of any matter, cause or thing whatsoever, as a result of said Peace Officer or Peace Officers recovering, holding, storing, or conveying, the above described vehicle, which I have this day reported as stolen and which is now out of my possession. This release and waiver will remain in effect until such time as above described vehicle shall be recovered and again be in my possession

Is vehicle community property?_____ Are you delinquent in payments?_____
SIGNATURE OF PERSON MAKING REPORT_____
SIGNED, OFFICER _____ Date_____ Hour _____

Illus. 28.
Vehicle Recovery Report. City of Sacramento, California.

AUTOMOBILE IMPOUND REPORT

	TOW REPORT NO.
	MPD 61958

Police Department – City of Minneapolis

License No. _____ Serial Number _____

Make _____ Body Style _____ Model / Year _____ _____

Date Recovered _____ 19____, _____ M   Recovered By _____

Where Recovered_____ On Street – Alley – Parking Lot – Used Car Lot – Garage – Yard

Recovered on Information From _____

Reason for Impounding_____ Stolen _____ Accident _____ Burned_____ Stripped _____

Extent of Damage to Vehicle _____   _____

Were Doors Locked?_____Ignition Locked?_____Trunk Locked?_____Were Keys in Car?_____

If City Property Was Damaged, indicate extent _____

Tow Truck Ordered At____M   Arrived At_____ M.   Tow Truck Driver's Name _____

Persons Suspected _____

Persons Arrested _____

Property in Vehicle:_____

Disposition of Property In Vehicle_____

Remarks _____

Towed By:_____ Report Made By Officer _____ Date & Time _____

AUTO DESK   DATE OF RELEASE: _____

!LL.

Illus. 29.

Recovery Report, Police Department, City of Minneapolis, Minnesota.

Form 3a—20M—11-65   SP*25906-257

TIME ____11:30 P.M.____

OFFICER'S REPORT

OREGON STATE POLICE

No. _____

Place ... __Salem__ _____

County _____ **Marion** _____

Subject __STOLEN VEHICLE__ _____

____June 28_____, 19_66_

'62 Chev. Sdn. Ore. 4N-6005, ID #1122334, red color

Reg. Owner - ROE, JOHN G., 1222 Main Street, Salem, Oregon

DOE, JOHN RAY - Suspect

At 11:10 P.M., June 28, 1966, owner called this office and reported above vehicle stolen from in front of his residence between 10:00 P.M. and 11:10 P.M. that date.

Keys were in vehicle and it contained approximately 2 gallons of gasoline, left tail light damaged.

Suspect John Ray Doe, WM, 19 years, 5'10", 170 lbs., brown hair, blue eyes, seen loitering near vehicle short time before theft.

At 11:15 P.M., June 28, 1966, the above theft was transmitted to local cars by radio and subject of APB #140 SMO at 11:20 P.M. same date.

613-21   JOHN LAWMAN, Pfc.

Illus. 30.

Officer's Recovery Report. Oregon State Police.

What?

What vehicle is being recovered?
What evidence was located?
What is the condition of the vehicle?
What is apparently missing?
What was found in the vehicle?
What direction was the vehicle parked when located?
What follow-up is required or requested?

Where?

Where was the auto recovered?

Where was the evidence located?

Where is the vehicle stored?

Where is the evidence stored?

Quite often stolen vehicles are abandoned near the place where it was stripped. When a thief takes a vehicle, he is reasonably certain its loss will not be discovered for some time; and if he drives it with reasonable care, he will go unnoticed. However, if the thief keeps the vehicle longer than just for quick use, he exposes himself to the risk of the vehicle becoming wanted and sought for. The thief will abandon it close to his destination in order to get himself off the streets and into his home or some other building. Should he be stopped by the police walking in a foreign neighborhood, chances of his being connected to the stolen vehicle are increased. If the stolen vehicle was stripped and the remains are being towed a great distance, chances are good a police officer may stop the suspects and check the vehicle. The thief must therefore, dispose of the stolen vehicle as soon as possible. The vehicle, in most cases, will be abandoned close to where the thief has terminated his use for it. The location **where** the vehicle is recovered is important for three reasons:

1. It may be close to the thief's whereabouts.
2. Recoveries should be plotted on a pin map to show pattern.
3. Area may be watched for those who work on autos.

When?

When was the vehicle recovered?
1. Time
2. Date

Who?

Who discovered the stolen vehicle?

Who reported the stolen vehicle?

Who recovered the stolen vehicle?

Who examined the stolen vehicle?

Who is a suspect?

Who are the witnesses?

Who is the owner or victim?

Who discovered the stolen vehicle and what brought his attention to it? When did he first observe it and under what circumstances? Did he see anyone in or near the vehicle? Does he know or can he identify the suspect? These are important questions and, when possible, the person who calls the police reporting the abandoned vehicle should be carefully interviewed. If a suspect emerges in the course of the investigation the report should indicate who implicates the suspect and his reasons for doing so.

How?

How was the vehicle taken to the location where it was abandoned?

Was it driven? Was it pushed or towed?

All vehicles with the steering wheel and shifting lever locking device should be examined at the rear bumper and rear axle housings or rear springs for signs a tow truck had raised the rear of the vehicle in order to tow it away. If there are no such signs present, strong suspicion should be placed on the vehicle having been driven to this location and that a key had been used to unlock the steering wheel and the transmission shifting lever. How was the suspect developed?

Why?

Generally, **why** the vehicle was stolen, is answered by it's recovery.

If it is recovered in one piece, it was used for joy riding or transportation. If the vehicle is recovered stripped, it was stolen for the parts.

In preparing a recovery report the officer should inventory the entire contents of the vehicle. A notation should be made of those items obviously removed (engine, transmission, battery, etc.) The inventory should extend to the trunk area also when it is possible to enter it. Two very important reasons for this are:

1. This gives the officer an accurate record of what was in the vehicle when he found it and what may have been removed. Future court action or other investigation may depend on this.

2. Should the victim make a claim against an insurance company or police agency claiming the loss of many expensive items, the officer can show what was in the vehicle at the time he made the recovery report. Many such claims are frequently fraudulent and simply a trick to bilk the insurance company of money, or to falsely accuse the officer of taking the items. Therefore, when the officer can show he has taken reasonable steps to safeguard the property he lessens the possibility of criticism.

Identifying The Vehicle.

Generally there are four methods by which the identification of the vehicle is made possible.

License plates.

License plates, if displayed, are easiest to observe and check. However, because they may easily be switched or altered their reliability for positive identification is open to question.

Identification or engine numbers.

This is the most reliable means of identifying a vehicle. Examination of this number should be made to determine if it has been altered or removed. Use this number when checking out of state vehicles for **wants**.

Personal identification of the vehicle by the owner.

Identification through general description and personal knowledge of specific features. The owner may be able to identify his vehicle by color, color combination, former color, body style, upholstery, papers, scratches, repairs, damaged areas, broken or cracked glass, articles in the vehicle, etc.

Confidential numbers.

As a last resort, this method may be used by the auto theft specialist. Confidential numbers are identification numbers placed on vehicles in such places that are not in public view and can be referred to for positive identification should a question arise regarding the public vehicle identification number.

Recovering the Stolen Vehicle with Occupants.

Should the officer observe a stolen vehicle with occupants, he should not attempt to apprehend them by himself. The officer should advise his radio dispatcher of the description of the stolen vehicle, and of his location, and make a request for assistance. If possible, follow the stolen vehicle without arousing the suspects' suspicions. Make every effort not to have the suspects attempt to elude the officer with a high-speed chase. Be alert and prepared for any sudden movements. If the vehicle is wanted, the officer should have reason to believe the occupants are wanted also. Remember, the occupants may not be just "joy-riding kids" but criminals fleeing from another crime. By the same token, the vehicle may have been wanted but is no longer wanted and someone neglected to cancel the **want.**

Stop When it is Unknown as to Whether Vehicle is Wanted.

Officers will not always be provided with knowledge that the vehicle about to be stopped is stolen or wanted. It is in these instances where danger is para-mount. The officer is about to stop a vehicle for a traffic violation or because he believes its occupants are acting suspiciously. He has first requested a "want check" with his radio dispatcher on the license plate displayed on the vehicle. The reply is "no wants at this time". This does not necessarily mean that the vehicle is not wanted; the license plate may be cold (unwanted), or possibly the crime has not yet been brought to the attention of the police.

Making the Stop.

The officer should pick the spot, when possible, to stop the suspect vehicle. If it is night, a well lighted location should be chosen if possible. The stop should be made away from an intersection where the suspect could make an escape on foot. The officer should give attention to the flow of traffic in order that the stop may cause no traffic hazard. The officer must be alert for anything being discarded from the vehicle, as it may be usable as evidence. It may also be advisable to inform the radio dispatcher of the intended stop, give a brief description of the vehicle, its occupants, reason for the stop, and location of the stop.

The stop is made and the officer prepares to approach the stopped vehicle which contains several individuals. A good policy for the officer to practice is to **remove the keys from the police vehicle.** Making traffic stops day in and day out often causes officers to fall into a routine which, more often than not, results in the officers' relaxing their guard. Remember, **there is no such thing as a routine stop.** Every stop will differ.

In approaching the stopped vehicle, the officer should have his attention directed at the occupants for any sudden movements. The person who makes the first aggressive movement usually has the advantage. Remember, he who has committed a crime knows what he has done. He does not know how much the officer knows or may not know why he is being stopped. There comes to mind, at this point, an incident that took place not long ago. An officer pursued a vehicle across open country in the late evening hours for what appeared to be a speed violation. The pursuit reached speeds in excess of one hundred miles an hour and continued for several miles. Suddenly the speeder stopped, as did the officer behind him. The officer, apparently feeling he had "just another speeder" approached the vehicle with citation book in one hand and his flashlight in the other. Suddenly the "speed violator" jumped from his vehicle, shot the officer to death, and drove away. As it turned out, the "speed violator" had held up a store and was driving a vehicle he had stolen earlier that day. The officer began his pursuit because he thought a speed violation had been committed, the suspect believed the officer was attempting to apprehend him for the hold up and the stolen vehicle. Being an exconvict, he did not want to be returned to prison, so he shot the officer in an effort to make good his escape. It can not be too urgently stressed that when making what appears to be a "routine stop", or any stop for that matter, that the approach to the vehicle be made with alertness and caution so that they may be in a position to take defensive action should the driver or any occupant of the stopped vehicle suddenly attack the officer.

"Sizing up" the situation BEFORE and AFTER the stop.

The officer must be on constant alert for some clue that will indicate the vehicle is stolen, or wanted in connection with another crime. He must "size up" the vehicle, its occupants, and the locality where the stop is to be made prior to making the stop. Assistance from another unit may be advisable and should be requested. Look over the vehicle and the occupants. Do they fit? As the officer approaches the vehicle he should watch the actions of all the occupants. Do they seem familiar with the vehicle? Particular attention should be directed towards the driver. Does he appear nervous or eager to meet the officer away from the vehicle? Has he turned off the ignition or is the engine running—perhaps in preparation to speed away as soon as the officer leaves his patrol vehicle.

Once at the stopped vehicle, the officer should quickly observe the ignition switch. Does it appear to be in order? After examining registration documents, do these appear in order? These and other steps must be completed to the satisfaction to the officer following which interviewing can take place.

11

VEHICLE IDENTIFICATION*

Familiarity with Vehicle Models, etc., essential.

A good investigator should provide himself with a thorough knowledge of vehicles, their stock appearance, how one model differs from another of the same make and year, the difference in makes from one year to another, how to identify these vehicles, and what accessories are factory installed. He should also be familiar with the location of the vehicle identification number, and how the factory affixed the number plate to the vehicle.

Methods of Affixing and Location of Identification Numbers.

Unfortunately not all vehicle manufacturers use standard means of affixing vehicle identification number plates to vehicles. Some vehicles, like the motor-

---

*Some of the information contained in chapter eleven was obtained through the courtesy of Mr. Eugene Halm, Manager of the Pacific Coast Division of the National Auto Theft Bureau, San Francisco, California. The N.A.T.B. is an organization established in 1912 by several automobile insurance companies which recognized the tremendous theft problem at that time and had the foresight to take steps to combat it. The organization grew from a few agents to many, now located throughout the United States, Canada, and Mexico. Calling these agents experts is not enough to describe their capabilities in this field. The information gathered by this organization far exceeds that which can be developed, retained, and disseminated by any local organization. Information regarding identification and numbering systems of vehicles has been accumulated from manufacturers by N.A.T.B. since the early 40's and made available to auto theft specialists throughout the world. N.A.T.B. publishes yearly current vehicle identification information in the form of a manual. The manual may be purchased through the Palmer Publishing Company, Downers Grove, Illinois. It is from these manuals that some of the identification numbering systems information for this book has been obtained. Physical examination of many vehicles by the author has also added a great deal to the information in this chapter.

cycle and pre 1955 automobiles, have the vehicle identification number stamped on the engine block. The
vehicle identification number of some trucks will be
found stamped on the frame, while other makes, like
many Ford Motor Company products, have this number stamped on the body panel. Still another method
employed is stamping the vehicle identification number on a metal plate and then affixing this plate to
the vehicle by means of rivets, screws, or spot welding.

Another problem area exists because vehicle manufacturers have not used a uniform location on which
to affix the vehicle identification number or number
plate. Considerable confusion results as to where the
officer should look in order to find the number and
identify the vehicle. Some locations used are door
posts, frame rails, the firewall, and on the engines. Although vehicle manufacturers are striving to stan-
dardize the location for vehicle identification numbers
on 1969 and newer model vehicles, the problem concerning older models and large commercial vehicles
still exists.

Body Serial Number Identification.

Up to and including 1954, most vehicle identification
numbers were located on the engine. The engine number oftentimes proved unreliable, as engines could be
changed with little effort, and many owners failed to
record the engine changes with the Department of
Motor Vehicles, resulting in incorrect and unrecorded
identification numbers for vehicles. The law requiring that the replacement engine number be recorded
with the Depaartment of Motor Vehicles (section 4161
California Vehicle Code) necessitated the vehicle owner's surrendering his ownership documents to that

agency, which, in turn, had to prepare and issue new documents reflecting the engine change. Few people complied with the law and not much in the way of enforcement was done. In 1954 most states changed their laws to require that 1955 and newer model vehicles be identified by the body serial number, known today as the vehicle identification number (V.I.N.). This system is not one hundred per cent in effect, as many manufacturers of motorcycles, large trucks and foreign vehicles deviate from this procedure.

As a guide, and with a fair amount of accuracy, the officer can rely on the following information while searching for the vehicle identification number:

1954 and older — Engine or frame number. (See Illus. 31)

1955 to some 1968 — Vehicle identification number plate affixed to the body. (See Illus. 32)

Most 1968 to current year model — Vehicle identification number plate on dashboard inside of the windshield. (See Illus. 33)

Illus. 31.
Engine or frame number prior to 1954.

Illus. 32.
Vehicle identification number affixed to the body.

Illus. 33

Various locations at which vehicle identification number may be found on most vehicles since 1968.

The Vehicle Identification Number.

What is a vehicle identification number? It is the number assigned to a vehicle by the manufacturer for the purpose of distinguishing one vehicle from another. In some states, an agency, usually a state police agency, has the authority to issue replacement vehicle identification numbers to those vehicles whose original factory vehicle identification number has been removed. This same agency may also issue a vehicle identification number to a home made type vehicle such as a hot rod or custom type vehicle. Although this may be the best means of identification, it is not the only means, as will be discussed later in this chapter.

The vehicle identification number is usually made up of a combination of numbers or numbers and letters. In many cases these combinations will offer a very good description of the vehicle.

Illus. 34.
Vehicle identification number for a 1968 Dodge.

Examples Showing Information Revealed by Identification Number.

For example illustration 34 vehicle identification number for a 1968 Dodge, DK41L8D250931, reveals the following information about this vehicle.

D. Dodge (make of vehicle).

K. Police special (Series).

41. 4 door sedan (body style).

L. V8, 440 cubic inch, high performance engine (engine description).

8. 1968 model (year designator).

D. Belvidere, Illinois (assembly plant).

250931. Sequential production number.

Similarly, the vehicle identification number for a 1970 Ford, OG73H100001, will reveal the following:

O. 1970 (year designator).

G. Chicago, Illinois (assembly plant).

73. 4 door, 2 seat, Country Sedan, station wagon (body style)

H. 351 cubic inch, V8, 2 barrel carburetor engine (engine description)

100001. Sequential production number.

A 1969 Chevrolet vehicle identification number, 164469L123456, provides the following:

1. Chevrolet (make designator).

6446. Chevrolet Kingswood model, 4 door, 3 seat, station wagon, with 6 cylinder engine with dual action tail gate (body style).

9. 1969 (year designator)

L. Los Angeles, California (assembly plant).

123456. Sequential production number.

A less descriptive vehicle identification system will be found on the Cadillac whose vehicle identification number, J0135679, provides the following:

J. 2 door coupe DeVille (model designator)

0. 1970 model (year designator)

135679. Sequential production number.

As indicated by the above examples, the information contained in the vehicle identification number plate of most vehicles will pretty well pin the vehicle down to a specific model. Careful examination of the plate itself, especially at the area around the spot welds or rivets, can offer evidence the plate has been tampered with—possibly removed from another vehicle. It is virtually impossible to remove the vehicle identification number plate from a vehicle without leaving some evidence of having done so. No alteration to it, regardless of the method used, will resemble the original factory application.

Vehicle Identification Number Plates and Vehicle Number Plates.

There is a great variance as to placement of **the vehicle identification** number plate or the **vehicle number plate** by the manufacturer. The **vehicle identification number plate** for most automobiles and light trucks manufactured from 1955 to 1967 should be

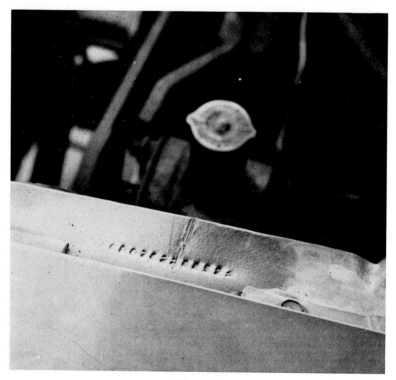

Illus. 35.
Vehicle number plate.

found screwed, riveted, or spot welded in the vicinity of the left front door hinge post. On others the identification number will be stamped onto the frame (for example the Cadillac) or into a body panel (for example Ford products, (see Illus. 35). **Vehicle number plates** screwed to the body of American made automobiles, such as the Cadillac or Ford products, ARE NOT the vehicle **identification number plates.** Cadillac refers to this plate as the lubrication record plate and Ford as a warranty plate. These plates may easily be removed, without much evidence of having done so, and therefore must NOT be relied upon, nor were they intended for use as the identification for that vehicle. These plates, however, should not be considered useless as they do contain certain information of value that can be used to help identify a vehicle. This area will be discussed later in this chapter. The **vehicle identification number plate** screwed onto the body of a large commercial vehicle and foreign vehicles, usually on the firewall in the engine compartment or inside the cab under the dashboard, may very well be the identification for that vehicle.

In 1968 automobile manufacturers changed the location of the **vehicle identification number plate** on most American made automobiles. Most placed this plate on the dashboard visible from the outside on the left corner. All Ford passenger cars came with the plate on the right side. A few did, however, retain other locations for the plate which do not differ from prior years. In 1969 most all automobile manufacturers in America and several foreign manufacturers placed the **vehicle identification number plate** on the dashboard visible from the outside on the left corner. 1970 and 1971 models have retained this location.

Engine Numbers

As mentioned earlier in this chapter, prior to 1954, engine number were used to identify the vehicle. Following the discontinuance of this method of identification, most vehicle manufacturers ceased stamping engines and transmissions with identifying numbers, with the exception of large commercial vehicles and motorcycles. This presented law enforcement agencies with another problem, as engines and transmissions — especially high performance engines and four speed transmissions — stolen from vehicles could not be identified. As these thefts increased, or rather skyrocketed, some manufacturers, particularly those experiencing the greatest problem, returned to stamping some of the engines and transmissions with identifying numbers. This was done mostly to the high performance type equipment, the target of the thieves. This, of course, was a big help to law enforcement agencies, as they were again able to identify stolen components. Although it did not take long for the auto thieves to learn of these identification numbers and to develop means to obliterate them (Illus. 36 engine number having been ground off), law enforcement officers were able to recognize the obliterations (violation of sections 10750 and 10751 of the California Vehicle Code) and to develop methods of restoring the numbers.

Illus. 36.
Obliteration of identification numbers easily detected.

Illustration 37 is an example of the identification number of an engine block having been restored after it was ground off by a thief.

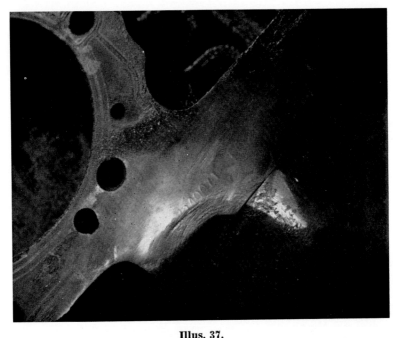

Illus. 37.

Example of restoration of identification number after it had been ground off.

Many motorcycles have both engine numbers and frame numbers. One exception is the Harley Davidson motorcycle, which, until 1969, had an engine number only that was used for identification purposes. From 1970 on both the engine and the frame have been numbered. Some motorcycles have engine numbers and frame numbers which are the same; others do not. When making a want check on a motorcycle, always check both numbers, if possible. Generally the frame number is near the "goose neck", and the engine number is on the crankcase block. Disreputable motorcycle gangs have contributed greatly to the motorcycle theft problem and are responsible for many of those stolen.

How to Detect Engine Number Alterations.

When the factory prepares the "boss" or pad upon which the engine number is to be stamped, the surface is machine ground even and smooth. Except for fine striations, uniform in pattern caused by the circular rotation of the grinding machine, there should be no other blemishes on this surface. The numbers are machine stamped on this surface at the factory, and are in a true line and evenly spaced. This would not be the same in an alteration. Regrinding may leave marks which will be course and straight or polished so that the surface is very smooth. The "boss" or pad will be ground in a cup shape and it is unlikely numbers restamped will be in a straight line, evenly spaced, and true. The cup shape (low in the center) can be determined by laying a straight edge across the surface of the pad. The cupping is caused by the grinder cutting away numbers which were stamped away from the edges of the pad, towards the center, requiring more metal to be ground off here than at the edges.

To protect the engine number from alterations, and to aid law enforcement agencies in detecting an alteration, some manufacturers prepare the number pad with a unique pattern. For example, the Honda and Yamaha motorcycles have the engine number stamped on a pad which is corrugated (Illus. 38). Anyone grinding off the number would also remove the corrugation, resulting in an obvious alteration. Refer to Illus. 36.

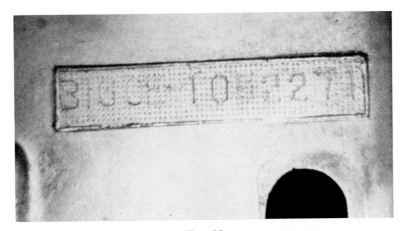

Illus. 38.
Corrugated pad on Honda and Yamaha motorcycles readily reveals any tampering with engine number.

When examining engines, transmissions, or other components for identification numbers, do not mistake casting or forging numbers, the firing order of the ignition system, or production numbers for them (Illus. 39).

Casting, Forging or Firing Numbers.

Casting or forging numbers and the firing order are numbers which will be RAISED on the cast item while the production number will be stamped INTO the casting resembling an identification number. All identification numbers are stamped INTO the component. The production number is a number that the factory stamps into the component which identifies the plant where the component was manufactured or assembled, the date it was manufactured or assembled, and perhaps the plant inspectors code. This number is not used for identification purposes. Numbers used for the identification of components are usually a repeat of the complete vehicle identification number or

Illus. 39.
Example of casting, forging or firing number.

a partial repeat of the vehicle identification number for the vehicle from which the component came.

Examine the Vehicle Identification Number Plate for Alterations or Other Signs of Tampering.

Examine the vehicle identification number plate for signs of tampering or that it has been altered. Such evidence as scratch marks about the face of the plate, or bent edges of the plate, or if the plate is being held in place by screws, when it should be fastened with rivets or spot welds, is an indication that a good possibility exists that the true identity of the vehicle is being concealed and that the vehicle may be stolen.

Some identification number plates have been removed from one vehicle and attached to another by the use of glue, tar, epoxy, or chewing gum. When this method is used, a small space between the vehicle body and the identification number plate will be evident which, normally, would not be present in a factory installation of the plate. A little pull from under the plate with the fingernail or a small pocket knife will reveal if this was done as the plate will readily come off. Care must be exercised not to re-

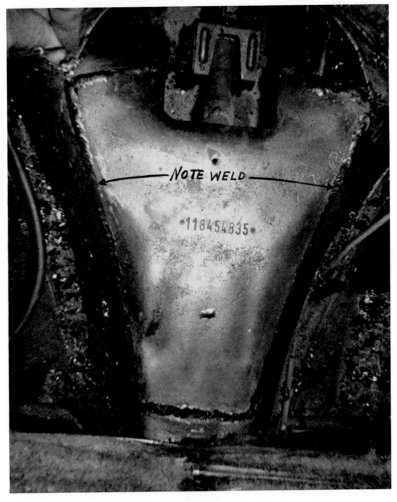

Illus. 40.

"Number transplant." Illustration shows the body panel with a replacement number welded in place of the original number. Note weld around edges not found on original panel.

Illus. 41

Example of an error in original stamping of identification number, voiding of that number by use of letter "v" before and after voided number and the imprinting of the correct number.

move a good plate from the vehicle. Identification numbers that are stamped into the body panel would require that the body panel from one vehicle be cut out and welded into another. (Illus. 40) A little closer scrutiny will reveal this. In these cases the auto theft specialist should be contacted as he will be able to identify the vehicle by other means.

There are instances where the factory will stamp an identification number onto a vehicle in error. In the case of the 1967 Ford in illustration (Illus. 41) the factory erred when placing the original number on the body panel. In order to correct this and to avoid having an obvious obliteration, the incorrect number was stamped with the letter "V" before and after the incorrect number, denoting it has been voided by the factory, and that the correct number was stamped along side of it. Note that the restamped number is hand stamped, not in straight and even alignment.

The theft of large commercial vehicles—trucks, tractors and trailers—is mounting and the recovery rate is very low. Some of the rigs are altered; identifying items from other vehicles, old or wrecked, are placed on the stolen equipment and then repainted in an effort to conceal them. Other vehicles are stripped of all usable parts, and these parts are reused on many

Illus. 42.
Fictitious vehicle identification plate.

different rigs so as not to have too many items from one stolen rig on another. Some thieves, having become proficient in the art of the theft of commercial vehicles, make their own vehicle identification number plates (Illus. 42) and stamp fictitious numbers upon them. Then, with fictitious bills of sale, the rigs are reregistered. Note true vehicle identification plate of illustration (Illus. 43).

Supplemental Vehicle Identification Number Plates.

Supplemental vehicle identification number plates or numbers are those issued by the Department of Motor Vehicles when the manufacturers plate has been lost or destroyed.

Originally, the California Department of Motor Vehicles assigned a number prefixed by "DRF" (Illus. 44). This number was stamped onto the engine or frame of the vehicle and thereafter used as the vehicle identification number, by authority of section 4166 of the California Vehicle Code. The department would only issue such a number following receipt of satisfactory evidence of the identity and ownership of the vehicle.

In an effort to upgrade the system and to prevent illegal misuse of an assigned number, a new system was introduced in August 1970, whereby provision is made for a new vehicle identification plate to be issued upon which a number is placed prior to affixing it to the vehicle. Additionally the procedure followed in issuing the new plate is slightly different than in the past. Henceforth, the vehicle is inspected by an investigator of the California Highway Patrol, who makes an effort to identify the true identification

number. If this can be accomplished the original number is repeated on the new plate, followed by the

Illus. 43.
Courtesy Utility Trailer Company, Sacramento, California
Authentic vehicle identification plate.

Illus. 44.
An assigned number prefixed by the letters DRF as previously issued
by the California Department of Motor Vehicles.

suffix "CA" (Illus. 45). If the true identification
number cannot be determined, an investigation is in-
itiated to make certain that all supporting documents
of ownership are authentic, and that the vehicle is not

stolen. After this investigation is completed, a new number is assigned on a new identification plate. The number for such a vehicle and for a newly constructed vehicle will consist of the three letters "DMV", five numerals, followed by the letters "CA" (Illus. 46).

The new vehicle identification plate is made of anodized aluminum with an adhesive backing, so that it will adhere to the body or engine. In addition, two rivets are used to assure the plate cannot be removed. A logo or seal is also used to make an impression on the plate which outlines the State of California. The impression overlaps the end of the plate onto the frame or engine. The plate cannot be removed without being destroyed.

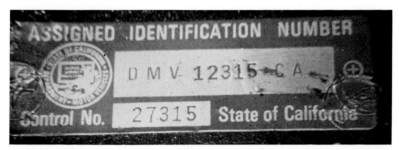

Illus. 45.
An assigned identification number issued by the California Department of Motor Vehicles as of August, 1970.

The information contained on the following pages consists of information that the officer can use to identify vehicles. Since pre 1960 vehicles, except for Chevrolet vehicles, are not really much of a theft problem, and few are still in operation, the information is mainly directed at post 1960 models. To list all the vehicles ever manufactured would be a tremendous task, however most American and the popular imports are included.

Illus. 46.
The new assigned vehicle identification number.

Location of Public Vehicle Identification Numbers

As mentioned earlier in this chapter, the vehicle identification number for pre 1955 vehicles should be found either on the firewall, engine block, or frame rail under the hood. Since very few of these vehicles are still in existence, and since they do not really pose a theft problem, no more need be mentioned about them. The following information, therefore, will pertain to 1955 to 1971 passenger vehicles.

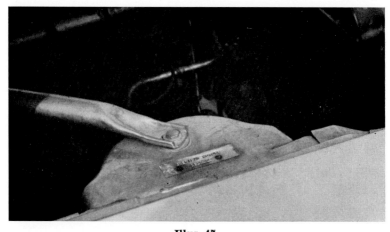

Illus. 47.
Location of vehicle identification numbers on American Motors vehicles.

AMERICAN MOTORS

AMBASSADOR	GREMLIN	RAMBLER
AMERICAN	HORNET	REBEL
AMX	JAVELIN	SST
DPL	MARLIN	

1955 to 1958: V.I.N. plate is spot welded to the firewall on the right side under the hood.

1959 to 1968: V.I.N. plate spot welded to the top of the right front wheel panel under the hood. (Illus. 47)

1959 to 1964.
Sample V.I.N. plate with number:

```
AMERICAN MOTORS
     M123468
```

First letter (M) designates the series.
The last six numbers are the sequential production numbers.

SERIES		1959 SERIES DESIGNATOR	1960	1961	1962	1963	1964
Ambassador	V8	D	C	—	—	—	—
American	6	A	A	—	—	—	—
Classic	V8	M	B	B	B	B	B
Classic	6	V	H	H	H	H	H
Rambler	6	—	—	C	C	G	G
Rebel	V8	—	—	A	—	Z	Z

1965.
Sample V. I. N. plate with number:

```
AMERICAN MOTORS
     Z123456
```

The first letter (Z) designates the series and engine type.
The last six numbers are the sequential production numbers.

SERIES			SERIES DESIGNATOR
Ambassador	232	6	S
	287	V8	E
	327	V8	H
American	196 OHV	6	P
	232	6	W
Classic	199	6	J
	232	6	L
	287	V8	Z
	327	V8	U

1966 and 1967.

Sample V. I. N. plate and number:

```
┌─────────────────────────┐
│     AMERICAN MOTORS      │
│     A6KF97H123456        │
└─────────────────────────┘
```

First letter (A) designates American Motors.
Second number designates the year model

6 — 1966   7 — 1967

Third letter designates the assembly plant.
K   Kenosha, Wisc.
B   Bramtpon, Ontario, Canada

Fourth letter designates the transmission.
A   Automatic 3 speed with column shift
C   Automatic 3 speed with floor shift
F   4 speed with floor shift
O   Standard 3 speed with column shift and overdrive
S   Standard 3 speed with column shift

Fifth number (9) designates body style.
5   4 Dr Sdn
6   2 Dr Sdn
7   2 Dr Convertible
8   Station Wagon
9   2 Dr Hard Top Coupe

Sixth number (7) designates body series.
0   Rambler American 220
0   Rambler Classic 550
2   Ambassador 880
5   Ambassador 990
5   Rambler American 440
5   Rambler Classic 770
7   Rambler American Rogue
7   Rambler Classic Rebel
7   Ambassador DPL
7   Marlin

Seventh letter (H) designates engine description.

A	American	6 — 199 — 1V Carb
B	American	6 — 232 — 2V Carb
F	Classic	6 — 232 — 1V Carb
G	Classic	6 — 232 — 2V Carb
H	Classic	V8 — 287 — 2V Carb
J	Classic	V8 — 327 — 2V Carb
K	Classic	V8 — 327 — 4V Carb
M	Ambassador	6 — 232 — 2V Carb
N	Ambassador	V8 — 287 — 2V Carb
P	Ambassador	V8 — 327 — 2V Carb
Q	Ambassador	V8 — 327 — 4V Carb

Seventh letter (H) designates engine description.

V	Marlin	6 — 232 — 1V Carb
S	Marlin	6 — 232 — 2V Carb
T	Marlin	V8 — 287 — 2V Carb
U	Marlin	V8 — 327 — 4V Carb
W	Marlin	V8 — 327 — 2V Carb

The last six numbers are the sequential production numbers.

1968 — 1969 — 1970 — 1971

Sample V.I.N. plate with number:

```
┌─────────────────────────────┐
│                             │
│       A9S162B1123456        │
│                             │
└─────────────────────────────┘
```

Some 1968 models have the V.I.N. plate spot welded to the top of the right front wheel panel under the hood while other 1968, 1969, to 1971 models have the VIN plate on the dashboard visible through the windshield from the outside on the left side. (Illus. 33 at B)

First letter (A) designates American Motors.
Second number designates year model.
8 — 1968   9 — 1969   0 — 1970   1 — 1971

Third letter (S) designates transmission type.

A	Automatic 3 speed column shift
C	Automatic 3 speed floor shift (1968)
C	Standard 3 speed floor shift (1969)
C	Automatic console shift (1970)
M	4 speed floor shift
O	Standard 3 speed column shift with overdrive (1968)
S	Standard 3 speed column shift
S	Standard 3 speeed floor shift on 1970 Javelin

Fourth number designates series (1).

0	American
0	Hornet (1970)
1	Rebel
3	AMX
7	Javelin
8	Ambassador

Fifth number (6) designates body style.

5	4 Dr Sdn	7	Convrt (1968)
6	2 Dr Sdn	8	Station Wagon

Sixth number (2) designates body series.

0	1968 American 220; 1968, 1969, 1970 Rebel 550 Basic; 1970 Hornet Basic.
2	1968 Ambassador 880; 1969, 1970 Ambassador.
5	1968, 1969 American 440; 1968 Rebel 770; 1969, 1970 Javelin Hard Top; 1969, 1970 DPL; 1968 Ambassador 990.
7	1968, 1969 American Rogue; 1968, 1969, 1970 Rebel SST; 1968, 1969, 1970 AMX Hard Top; 1968 Javelin Hard Top; 1969, 1970 Javelin SST; 1968 Ambassador DPL; 1969, 1970 Ambassador SST; 1970 Hornet SST.

Seventh letter (B) designates engine style.

A	1968, 1969, 1970	6 — 199 — 1V Carb
B	1970	6 — 199 — 1V Carb
C	1968, 1969	6 — 232 — 2V Carb
E	1970	6 — 232 — 1V Carb
F	1970	6 — 232 — 1V Carb
G	1970	6 — 232 — 2V Carb
H	1970	V8 — 304 — 2V Carb
I	1970	V8 — 304 — 2V Carb
M	1968, 1969	V8 — 290 — 2V Carb
M	1970	V8 — 304 — 4V Carb
N	1968, 1969	V8 — 290 — 4V Carb
N	1970	V8 — 360 — 2V Carb
P	1970	V8 — 360 — 4V Carb
S	1968, 1969	V8 — 343 — 2V Carb
S	1970	V8 — 390 — 2V Carb
T	1968, 1969	V8 — 343 — 4V Carb
W	1968, 1969	V8 — 390 — 2V Carb
X	1968, 1969, 1970	V8 — 390 — 4V Carb

Eighth number (1) designates assembly plant.

1 to 6   Kenosha, Wisc
7 to 9   Brampton, Ontario, Canada

The last five numbers are the sequential production numbers.

BUICK

1955 to 1964. The V.I.N. plate is spot welded to the left front door hinge post. (Illus. 32)

1961 Special. V.I.N. is stamped into the body brace which extends from the firewall to the fender panel, left side, under the hood. (Illus. 48 at C)

1963 Riviera. V.I.N. plate is spot welded on top of the cowl on the right side under the hood. (Illus. 48 at A)

1964 Riviera. V.I.N. plate is spot welded on top of the cowl on the left side under the hood (Illus. 48 at B)

1965 to 1967. V.I.N. plate is riveted to the left front door hinge post. (Illus. 32)

1968 to 1971. V.I.N. plate is located on left side of the dashboard visible through the windshield. (Illus. 33 at B)

Assembly plants and their symbol designators.

1	Flint, Mich 1960 to 1964
2	Southgate, Calif 1960 to 1964
3	Linden, N.J. 1960 to 1963
3	Fremont, Calif 1964 only
4	Kansas City, Kan 1960 to 1964
5	Wilmington, Del 1960 to 1964
6	Atlanta, Ga 1960 to 1964
7	Baltimore, Md 1963 to 1964
7	Farmingham, Mass 1960 to 1962
8	Arlington, Tex 1960 to 1962

Illus. 48

Location of vehicle identification numbers on General Motors vehicles
— Buick division.

B   Baltimore, Md   1965 to 1968
C   Southgate, Calif   1965 to 1970
D   Atlanta, Ga   1965
D   Doraville, Ga   1966 to 1970
G   Farmingham, Mass   1966 to 1970
H   Flint, Mich   1965 to 1970
I   Oshash, Ontario, Canada   1966 to 1969
K   Kansas City, Mo   1965
X   Kansas City, Kan   1965 to 1970
Y   Wilmington, Del   1965 to 1970
Z   Fremont, Calif   1965 to 1970

1960.

Sample V.I.N. plate with number:

```
┌─────────────────────────────┐
│            BUICK            │
│          4B1123456          │
└─────────────────────────────┘
```

First number designates the series model.

4	La Sabre	4400 series
6	Invicta	4600 series
7	Electra	4700 series
8	Electra	4800 series

Second letter designates the year model.
G   1960

Third number designates the assembly plant.

The last six numbers are the sequential production numbers.

1961.

V.I.N. plate same as 1960.

First number designates the series model.

0	Special	4000 series
1	Special	4100 series
4	La Sabre	4400 series
6	Invicta	4600 series
7	Electra	4700 series
8	Electra 225	4800 series

Second letter designates the year model.
H   1961

Third number designates the assembly plant.

The last six numbers are the sequential production numbers.

1962.

V.I.N. plate same as 1960.

First number or letter designates the series model.

A	Special V6	4000 series
0	Special V8	4000 series
1	Special	4100 series
3	Special Skylark	4300 series
4	La Sabre	4400 series
6	Invicta	4600 series
8	Electra	4800 series

Second letter designates the year model.
I   1962

Third number designates the assembly plant.

The last six numbers are the sequential production numbers.

1963 and 1964.

V.I.N. plate same as 1960 to 1962 models.

First letter or number designates the series.

A	Special V6	4000
O	Special V8	4000
B	Special V6	4100
1	Special V8	4100
C	Special Skylark V6	4300 (1964) (None for 1963)
3	Special Skylark V8	4300
4	La Sabre V8	4400
6	Invicta V8	4600
6	Wildcat V8	4600
7	Riviera V8	4600 and 4700
8	Electra 225 V8	4800

Second letter designates the year model.

J   1963
K   1964

Third number designates the assembly plant.

The last six numbers are the sequential production numbers.

1965.

Sample V.I.N. plate with number:

1965
to
1967

BUICK
433695B123456

First number designates the Buick automobile.

4   Buick division of G.M.C.

The next four numbers designate body style.

Body Style	6 Cyl Series	V8 Series
Special		
2 dr cpe	3327	3427
4 dr sdn	3369	3469
Convert	3367	3467
4 dr S.W. 6 pass	3335	3435
Special Deluxe		
4 dr sdn	3569	3669
4 dr S.W. 6 pass	3535	3635
Sportwagon		
4 dr S.W. 6 pass	—	4255
4 dr S.W. 9 pass	—	4265
Sportwagon Deluxe		
4 dr S.W. 6 pass	—	4455
4 dr S.W. 9 pass	—	4465

Body Style	6 Cyl Series	V8 Series
Skylark		
2 dr cpe	4327	4427
2 dr hard top	4337	4437
4 dr sdn	4369	4469
Convert	4367	4467
La Sabre		
2 dr hard top	—	5237
4 dr sdn	—	5269
4 dr hard top sdn	—	5239
La Sabre Deluxe		
2 dr hard top	—	5437
4 dr sdn	—	5469
4 dr hard top sdn	—	5439
Convert	—	5467
Wildcat		
2 dr hard top	—	6237
4 dr sdn	—	6269
4 dr hard top sdn	—	6239
Wildcat Deluxe		
2 dr hard top	—	6437
4 dr sdn	—	6469
4 dr hard top sdn	—	6439
Convert	—	6464
Wildcat Custom		
2 dr hard top	—	6637
4 dr hard top sdn	—	6639
Convert	—	6667
Electra 225		
2 dr hard top	—	8237
4 dr sdn	—	8269
4 dr hard top sdn	—	8239
Electra 225 Deluxe		
2 dr hard top	—	8437
4 dr sdn	—	8469
4 dr hard top sdn	—	8439
Convert	—	8467
Riviera		
2 dr hard top	—	9447

Sixth number designates year model.
5   1965

Seventh letter designates assembly plant.

The last six numbers are the sequential production numbers.

1966 to 1971.
Sample V.I.N. plate with numbers:
1966 and 1967 same as 1965.

| 1968 to 1971 | 434360C123456 |

First number designates the Buick automobile.
4   Buick division of G.M.C.

The next four numbers designate the body style.

Body Style	1970	1969	1968	1967	1966	
			6 or V8		6	V8
Special						
2 dr cpe	—	—	—	3307	3307	3407
4 dr sdn	—	—	—	3369	3369	3469
Convert	—	—	—	—	3367	3467
4 dr S.W. 6 pass	—	—	—	3335	3335	3435
Special Deluxe						
2 dr cpe	—	3327	3327	—	3507	3607
2 dr hard top	—	—	—	3517	3517	3617
4 dr sdn	—	3369	3369	3569	3569	3669
4 dr S.W. 6 pass	—	3435	3435	3635	3535	3635
4 dr S.W. 6 pass with dual action tail gate	—	3436	—	—	—	—
Sportwagon						
4 dr S.W. 6 pass	3435	—	4455	4455	—	4255
4 dr S.W. 6 pass with dual action tail gate	3436	4456	—	—	—	—
4 dr S.W. 9 pass	—	—	4465	4465	—	4265
4 dr S.W. 9 pass with dual action tail gate	—	4466	—	—	—	—
Sportwagon Deluxe						
4 dr S.W. 6 pass	—	—	—	—	—	4455
4 dr S.W. 9 pass	—	—	—	—	—	4465
Sportwagon Wood grain finish						
4 dr S.W. 6 pass	—	—	—	4855	—	—
4 dr S.W. 9 pass	—	—	—	4865	—	—
Skylark						
2 dr cpe	3327	—	—	4307	4307	4407
2 dr hard top	—	3537	3537	4417	4317	4417
4 dr sdn	3369	3569	3569	—	—	—
4 dr hard top sdn	—	—	—	4439	4339	4439
Convert	—	—	—	4467	4367	4467
Skylark 350						
2 dr hard top	3537	—	—	—	—	—
4 dr sdn	3569	—	—	—	—	—

Body Style	1970	1969	1968	1967	1966 6	V8
			6 or V8			
Skylark Custom						
2 dr hard top	4437	4437	4437	—	—	—
4 dr sdn	4469	4469	4469	—	—	—
4 dr hard top sdn	4439	4439	4439	—	—	—
4 dr convert	4467	4467	4467	—	—	—
Skylark Grand Sport						
2 dr cpe	—	—	—	—	—	4607
2 dr hard top	--	—	—	—	—	4617
Convert	—	--	—	—	—	4667
G.S.						
2 dr hard top	3437	—	—	—	—	—
G.S. 350						
2 dr hard top	—	3437	3437	—	—	—
G.S. 455						
2 dr hard top	4637	—	—	—	—	—
Convert	4667	—	—	—	—	—
G.S. 400						
2 dr cpe	—	—	—	4607	—	—
2 dr hard top	—	4637	4637	4617	—	—
Convert	—	4667	4667	4667	—	—
La Sabre						
2 dr hard top	5237	5237	5287	5287	—	5237
4 dr sdn	5269	5269	5269	5269	—	5269
4 dr hard top sdn	5239	5239	5239	5239	—	5239
La Sabre Custom						
2 dr hard top	5437	5437	5487	5487	—	5437
4 dr sdn	5469	5469	5469	5469	—	5469
4 dr hard top sdn	5439	5439	5439	5439	—	5439
Convert	5467	5467	5467	5467	—	5467
La Sabre 455						
2 dr hard top	6437	—	—	—	—	—
4 dr sdn	6469	—	—	—	—	—
4 dr hard top sdn	6439	—	—	—	—	—
Wildcat						
2 dr hard top	—	6437	6487	6287	—	6237
4 dr sdn	—	6469	6469	6269	—	6269
4 dr hard top sdn	—	6439	6439	6239	—	6239
Convert	—	—	—	6267	—	6267
Wildcat Custom						
2 dr hard top	6637	6637	6687	6687	—	6637
4 dr hard top sdn	6639	6639	6639	6639	—	6639
Convert	6667	6667	6667	6667	—	6667
Estate Wagon						
4 dr 2 seat SW	6036	—	—	—	—	—
4 dr 3 seat SW	6046	—	—	—	—	—

Body Style	1970	1969	1968	1967	1966	
			6 or V8		6	V8
Electra 225						
2 dr hard top	8257	8257	8257	8257	—	8237
4 dr sdn	8269	8269	8269	8269	—	8269
4 dr hard top sdn	8239	8239	8239	8239	—	8239
Electra 225 Custom						
2 dr hard top	8457	8457	8457	8457	—	8437
4 dr sdn	8469	8469	8469	8469	—	8469
4 dr hard top sdn	8439	8439	8439	8439	—	8439
Convert	8467	8467	8467	8467	—	8467
Riviera						
2 dr hard top	9487	9487	9487	9487	—	9487

The sixth number designates the year model.

6	1966	8	1968	0	1970
7	1967	9	1969	1	1971

Seventh letter designates the assembly plant.

The last six numbers are the sequential production numbers.

CADILLAC

1955 to 1958. V.I.N. stamped on frame, right side, at vicinity opposite rear of engine.

1959 to 1962. V.I.N. stamped on frame, left side, at vicinity opposite radiator saddle.

1963 to 1964. V.I.N. stamped on frame, left side, at the cross member, forward of radiator saddle.

1965 to 1967. V.I.N. stamped on frame, right side, at vicinity under the battery box.

1967 El Dorado model. V.I.N. stamped on frame, left side, back of the radiator saddle.

Engine has a repeat of the V.I.N. also.

1968 to 1970. The V.I.N. plate is located on the left windshield post visible through the windshiedl (Ill. 33C).

1971. V.I.N. is located on the left side of the dashboard visible through the windshield (Ill. 33B).

The engine sand transmissions of 1968 to 1971 models are also stamped with a partial repeat of the V.I.N.

NOTE: The plastic plate found screwed to the left front door striked post bearing the V.I.N. should NOT be used for identification purposes.

1958 to 1964.

Sample V.I.N. The asterisks are included to protect the number.

63N123456

First and second numbers designate the year model.

58	1958	62	1962
59	1959	63	1963
60	1960	64	1964
61	1961		

The third letter designates the body style.

Ltr.	Body Style	Year Models						
A	4 dr sdn 4w	—	—	60	61	62	63	64
A	Sdn short deck	—	—	—	—	62	63	—
B	Sdn De Ville 4 dr 4W	—	—	60	61	62	63	64
C	Park Ave Sdn	—	—	—	—	—	63	—
E	ElDorado Biarritz Convert	58	59	60	61	62	63	64
F	2 dr Convert	58	59	60	61	62	63	64
G	2dr Hard Top	58	59	60	61	—	63	64
H	ElDorado Seville 2 dr cpe	58	59	60	—	—	—	—
H	ElDorado Convert DeVille	—	—	60	—	—	—	—
J	2 dr cpe DeVille	58	59	60	61	62	63	64
K	Hard top sdn	58	59	—	—	—	—	—
K	4 dr sdn 6W	—	—	60	61	62	63	64
L	4 dr Sdn DeVille	58	59	—	—	—	—	—
L	4 dr Sdn DeVille 6W	—	—	60	61	62	63	64
M	4 dr sdn 60 Special	58	59	60	61	62	63	64
N	4 dr sdn extended deck	58	—	—	—	—	—	—
N	4 dr hard top sdn 4W	—	—	—	—	62	63	64
P	4 dr ElDorado 70 Brougham	58	59	60	—	—	—	—
R	4 dr sdn Fleetwood 75	—	—	60	61	62	63	64
S	4 dr sdn 75 Imperial	58	59	—	—	—	—	—
S	Fleetwood limousine Imperial 75	—	—	60	61	62	63	64
Z	86 commercial chassis	58	59	60	61	62	63	64

The last six numbers are the sequential production numbers.

1965 to 1970.
Sample of 1968 to 1970 V.I.N. plate with number:

N0123456

First letter designates series model.

B	4 dr hard top sdn DeVille	65	66	67	68	69	70
E	Fleetwood ElDorado Convert	65	66	—	—	—	—
F	2 dr DeVille Convert	65	66	67	68	69	70
G	2 dr cpe Calais	65	66	67	68	69	70
H	2 dr ht cpe Fleetwood ElDorado	—	—	67	68	69	70
J	2 dr cpe DeVille	65	66	67	—	—	—
K	4 dr sdn Calais	65	66	67	68	69	70
L	4 dr sdn DeVille	65	66	67	68	69	70
M	4 dr sdn Fleetwood 60 Special	65	66	67	68	69	70
M	Fleetwood 60 Special Brougham	65	66	67	68	69	70
N	4 dr ht sdn Calais	65	66	67	68	69	70
P	Fleetwood 60 Special Brougham	—	66	67	68	69	70
R	Fleetwood 75 4 dr sdn	65	66	67	68	69	70
S	Fleetwood 75 4 dr sdn limousine	65	66	67	68	69	70

Second number designates the year model.

| 5 | 1965 | 7 | 1967 | 9 | 1969 |
| 6 | 1966 | 8 | 1968 | 0 | 1970 |

The last six numbers are the sequential production numbers.

1971.

Sample V.I.N.

683471Q123456

6   Cadillac division of G.M.C.

The next four numbers designate the body style and series.

Illus. 49

Vehicle identification number on Corvette (1960-1962) is spot welded to the steering column jacket under hood.

Sixth numbeer designates the year model.
1   1971

Seventh letter designates the assembly plant.
E   Linden, N.J.
Q   Detroit, Mich

The lats six numbers are the sequential production numbers.

Illus. 50

1963 to 1967 Corvette vehicle identification number riveted to body brace under the dashboard.

Illus. 51
Location of 1960 to 1964 Corvair vehicle identification number.

Illus. 52
Location of vehicle identification number on 1965 to 1967 Corvair.

CHECKER

1965 to 1967. V.I.N. plate is located screwed to the firewall, left side, under the hood.

1968 to 1971. V.I.N. plate is located on the left side of the dashboard visible through the windshield. (Ill. 33B).

Sample V.I.N. with number:

A12-1234-12345 V

Body style — A12

Sequential production number — 1234

Sequential production of chassis (Taxicab, Aerobus, etc.) — 12345

V designates it has V8 engine; no designator for 6 cyl. engine. — 12345

CHEVROLET

1955 to 1964. V.I.N. plate is spot welded to left front door hinge post. (Illus. 32)

1965 to 1967. V.I.N. plate is riveted to left front door hinge post. (Illus. 32)

1955 to 1959 Corvette. V.I.N. plate is screwed onto the left front door hinge post. (Illus. 32)

1960 to 1962 Corvette. V.I.N. plate is spot welded to the steering column jacket under hood. (Illus. 49)

1963 to 1967 Corvette. V.I.N. plate is riveted to body brace under the dashboard on the right side in the vehicle interior. (Illus. 50)

1960 to 1964 Corvair. V.I.N. plate is spot welded to the left front door striker plate post. (Illus. 51)

1965 to 1967 Corvair. V.I.N. plate is riveted to body panel in the engine compartment, to the left of the engine. (Illus. 52)

1968 to 1971. V.I.N. is located on the left side of the dashboard visible through the windshield. (Illus. 33 at B)

1968 to 1971 Corvette. V.I.N. is located on the left windshield post just above the dash. (Illus. 33 at C)

Assembly plants, their symbol designator and location.

A	Atlanta, Ga	1955 to 1970
B	Baltimore, Md	1955 to 1970
C	Atlanta, Ga	1964
C	Southgate, Calif	1965 to 1970
D	Atlanta, Ga	1965 to 1970
D	Doraville,	1968 to 1970
F	Flint, Mich	1955 to 1970
G	Farmingham, Mass	1960 to 1968
H	Freemont, Calif	1964
J	Janesville, Wisc	1955 to 1970
K	Kansas City, Kan	1955 to 1964
K	Kansas City, Mo	1965 to 1970
K	Leeds, Mo	1970
L	Lakewood, Ga	1970
L	Los Angeels, Calif	1955 to 1970
L	Van Nuys, Calif	1970
N	Norwood, Ohio	1955 to 1970
O	Oakland, Calif	1955 to 1963
R	Arlington, Tex	1963 to 1970
S	St. Louis, Mo	1955 to 1970
T	Tarrytown, N.Y.	1955 to 1970
U	Southgate, Calif	1964
U	Lordstown, Ohio	1966 to 1970
W	Willow Run, Mich	1960 to 1970
Y	Wilmington, ,Del	1955 to 1970
Z	Freemont, Calif	1965 to 1970
1	Oshawa, Ontario, Canada	1965 to 1970
2	Ste. Therese, Quebec, Canada	1965 to 1970

1955 to 1957.

Sample V.I.N. plate with number:

```
┌─────────────────────────────┐
│         CHEVROLET           │
│        VC56L123456          │
└─────────────────────────────┘
```

First or first and second letters designate the engine and body series.

A	6 Cyl	150 Series
VA	V8	150 Series
B	6 Cyl	210 Series
VB	V8	210 Series
C!	6 Cyl	Bel Air Series
VC	V8	Bel Air Series
D	6 Cyl	Sedan Delivery
VD	V8	Sedan Delivery
VE	V8	Corvette (1955 and 1956)
E	V8	Corvette (1957)

The next two numbers designate the year model.

55	1955
56	1956
57	1957

The next letter designates the assembly plant.

The last six numbers are the sequential production numbers.

1958

Sample V.I.N. plate with number:

```
┌─────────────────────────────┐
│         CHEVROLET           │
│        A58B123456           │
└─────────────────────────────┘
```

First letter designates engine and body series.

A	6 Cyl	Delray
B	V8	Delray
C	6 Cyl	Biscayne
D	V8	Biscayne
E	6 Cyl	Bel Air
F	V8	Bel Air
G	6 Cyl	Sedan Delivery
H	V8	Sedan Delivery
J	V8	Corvette

Second and third numbers designate the year model.

58	1958

Fourth letter designates the assembly plant. The letter designators for the 1958 model are the same aas those of the 1955 to 1957 models.

The last six numbers are the sequential production numbers.

1959.

V.I.N. plate same as 1958.

First letter designates engine and body series.

A   6 Cyl   Biscayne
B   V8   Biscayne
C   6 Cyl   Bel Air
D   V8   Bel Air
E   6 Cyl   Impala
F   V8   Impala
G   6 Cyl   Sedan Delivery and El Camino
H   V8   Sedan Delivery and El Camino
J   V8   Corvette

The second and third numbers designate the yeaar model.
59   1959

Fourth letter designates the assembly plant. The letter designators for the 1959 model are the same as those of the 1955 to 1958 models.

The last six numbers are the sequential production numbers.

1960 to 1964.

Sample V.I.N. plate with number:

```
┌─────────────────────────┐
│      CHEVROLET          │
│      31535D123456       │
└─────────────────────────┘
```

First number designates the year model.

0	1960	2	1962	4	1964
1	1961	3	1963		

The next four numbers designate the body style.

Body Style	1960 6 Cyl	1960 V8	1961 6	1961 8	1962 6	1962 8	1963 6	1963 8	1964 6	1964 8
Corvair										
2 dr cpe	0527	—	0527	—	—	—	—	—	—	—
4 dr sdn	0569	—	0569	—	—	—	—	—	—	—
4 dr sw	—	—	0535	—	—	—	—	—	—	—
Greeenbrier sw	—	—	R126	—	R126	—	R126	—	R126	—
Corvair Deluxe										
2 dr sdn	0727	—	—	—	—	—	—	—	—	—
4 dr sdn	0769	—	—	—	—	—	—	—	—	—

Body Style	1960 6 Cyl	1960 V8	1961 6	1961 8	1962 6	1962 8	1963 6	1963 8	1964 6	1964 8
Monza										
2 dr cpe	—	—	0927	—	—	—	—	—	—	—
4 dr sdn	—	—	0967	—	—	—	—	—	—	—
Spider cpe	—	—	—	—	—	—	—	—	0627	—
Spider cnvt	—	—	—	—	—	—	—	—	0667	—
500 2 dr cpe	—	—	—	—	0527	—	0527	—	0527	—
700 2 dr cpe	—	—	0727	—	0727	—	0727	—	—	—
4 dr sdn	—	—	0769	—	0769	—	0769	—	0769	—
4 dr sw	—	—	0735	—	0735	—	—	—	—	—
Monza 900										
2 dr sdn	—	—	—	—	0929	—	—	—	—	—
4 dr sdn	—	—	—	—	0969	—	0969	—	0969	—
4 dr sw	—	—	—	—	0935	—	0935	—	0935	—
Clb cpe	—	—	0927	—	—	—	0927	—	0927	—
Convrt	—	—	—	—	—	—	0967	—	0967	—

	1960 4 Cyl	1960 6 Cyl	1961 4	1961 6	1962 4	1962 6	1963 4	1963 6	1964 4	1964 6
Chev II										
100/200										
2 dr cpe	—	—	—	—	0111	0211	0111	0211	0111	0211
4 dr sdn	—	—	—	—	0169	0269	0169	0269	0169	0269
4 dr sw	—	—	—	—	0135	0235	0135	0235	0135	0235
300/400										
2 dr sdn	—	—	—	—	0311	0411	0311	0411	0311	0411
4 dr sdn	—	—	—	—	0369	0469	0369	0469	0369	0469
4 dr sw 3 seat	—	—	—	—	0345	0445	0345	0445	0345	0445
Nova 400										
2 dr sdn	—	—	—	—	—	0441	—	—	—	—
4 dr sdn	—	—	—	—	—	0449	—	0449	—	—
HT Cpe	—	—	—	—	—	0437	—	0437	—	—
Cnvrt	—	—	—	—	—	0467	—	0467	—	—
4 dr sw	—	—	—	—	—	0435	—	0435	—	0435

	1960 6 Cyl	1960 V8	1961 6	1961 8	1962 6	1962 8	1963 6	1963 8	1964 6	1964 8
Biscayne										
Sdn Utility	1121	1221	1121	1221	—	—	—	—	5580	5680
2 dr sdn	1111	1211	1111	1211	1111	1211	1111	1211	1111	1211
4 dr sdn	1119	1219	1169	1269	1169	1269	1169	1269	1169	1269
2 dr sw Brookwood	1115	1215	1135	1235	—	—	—	—	—	—
4 dr sw Brookwood	1135	1235	1145	1245	—	—	—	—	—	—
Biscayne Fleetmstr										
2 dr sdn	1311	1411	1311	1411	—	—	—	—	—	—
4 dr sdn	1319	1419	1369	1469	—	—	—	—	—	—

	1960 6 Cyl	1960 V8	1961 6	1961 8	1962 6	1962 8	1963 6	1963 8	1964 6	1964 8
Bel Air										
4 dr sw 6p	—	—	—	—	1535	1635	1535	1635	1535	1635
4 dr sw 9p	—	—	—	—	1545	1645	1545	1645	1545	1645
Bel Air										
2 dr sdn	1511	1611	1511	1611	1511	1611	1511	1611	1511	1611
4 dr sdn	1519	1619	1569	1669	1569	1669	1569	1669	1569	1669
2 dr HT	1537	1637	1537	1637	1537	1637	1537	1637	1537	1637
4 dr HT	1539	1639	1539	1639	—	—	—	—	—	—
4 dr sw 6p Parkwood	1535	1635	1535	1635	—	—	—	—	—	—
4 dr sw 9p Kingswood	1545	1645	1545	1645	—	—	—	—	—	—
Impala										
4 dr sdn	1719	1819	1769	1869	1769	1869	1769	1869	1769	1869
2 dr HT	1737	1837	1737	1837	1747	1847	1747	1847	1747	1847
4 dr HT	1739	1839	1739	1839	1739	1839	1739	1839	1739	1839
Cnvrt	1767	1867	1767	1867	1767	1867	1767	1867	1767	1867
Nomad sw 6 pass	1739	1835	1735	1835	—	—	—	—	—	—
Nomad sw 9 pass	—	—	1745	1845	—	—	—	—	—	—
2 dr sdn	—	—	1711	1811	—	—	—	—	—	—
4 dr sw 6p	—	—	—	—	1735	1835	1735	1835	1735	1835
4 dr sw 9p	—	—	—	—	1745	1845	1745	1845	1745	1845
Super Sport cpe	—	—	—	—	—	—	—	—	1347	1447
Super Sport convrt	—	—	—	—	—	—	—	—	1367	1467
Corvette Cpe	—	—	—	—	—	—	—	0837	—	0837
Convrt	—	0867	—	0867	—	0867	—	0867	—	0867
Chevelle 300										
2 dr sdn	—	—	—	—	—	—	—	—	5311	5411
4 dr sdn	—	—	—	—	—	—	—	—	5369	5469
2 dr sw	—	—	—	—	—	—	—	—	5315	5415
Malibu										
4 dr sw	—	—	—	—	—	—	—	—	5335	5435
2 dr HT	—	—	—	—	—	—	—	—	5537	5637
4 dr sdn	—	—	—	—	—	—	—	—	5569	5669
Convrt	—	—	—	—	—	—	—	—	5567	5667
2 seat sw	—	—	—	—	—	—	—	—	5535	5635
Malibu Super Sport										
3 seat sw	—	—	—	—	—	—	—	—	5545	5645
El Camino	—	—	—	—	—	—	—	—	5380	5480
Convrt	—	—	—	—	—	—	—	—	5767	5867
2 dr HT	—	—	—	—	—	—	—	—	5737	5837

The sixth letter designates the assembly plant.

The last six numbers are the sequential production numbers.

1965 to 1971.
Sample of V.I.N. plate with numbers:

1965
to
1967

```
┌─────────────────────────┐
│    CHEVROLET DD         │
│    136177G123456        │
└─────────────────────────┘
```

1968
to
1971

```
┌─────────────────────────┐
│    124870L123456        │
└─────────────────────────┘
```

First number designates the Chevrolet automobile.
1   Chevrolet division of G.M.C.

The next four numbers designate the body style.

Body Style	1965 4cyl	1965 6cyl	1966 4	1966 6	1967 4	1967 6	1968 4	1968 6	1969 4	1969 6	1970 4	1970 6
Corvair 500												
2 dr cpe	—	0137	—	0137	—	0137	—	0137	—	0137	—	—
4 dr sdn	—	0139	—	0139	—	—	—	—	—	—	—	—
Monza												
2 dr sdn	—	0537	—	0537	—	0537	—	0537	—	0537	—	—
4 dr sdn	—	0539	—	0539	—	0539	—	—	—	—	—	—
Convrt	—	0567	—	0567	—	0567	—	0567	—	0567	—	—
Corsa												
2 dr sdn	—	0730	—	0737	—	—	—	—	—	—	—	—
Convrt	—	0767	—	0767	—	—	—	—	—	—	—	—

	1965 4cyl	1965 6cyl	1965 V8	1966 4	1966 6	1966 8	1967	1968	1969	1970
Chevy 2 100										
2 dr sdn	1111	1311	1411	1111	1311	1411	—	—	—	—
4 dr sdn	1169	1369	1469	1169	1369	1469	—	—	—	—
4 dr sw 2 seat	—	1335	1435	—	1335	1435	—	—	—	—

	1965 6	1965 V8	1966 6	1966 V8	1967 6	1967 V8	1968 4	1968 6	1968 V8	1969 4	1969 6	1969 V8
Nova												
2 dr sdn	1537	1637	1537	1637	1537	1637	1127	1327	1427	1127	1327	1427
4 dr sdn	1569	1669	1569	1669	1569	1669	1169	1369	1469	1169	1369	1469
4 dr sw 2 seat	1535	1635	1535	1635	1535	1635	—	—	—	—	—	—

	1970 4	1970 6	1970 V8
Nova			
2 dr sdn	1127	1327	1427
4 dr sdn	1169	1369	1469
4 dr sw 2 seat	—	—	—

	1965 6	1965 V8	1966 6	1966 V8	1967 6	1967 V8	1968 6	1968 V8	1969 6	1969 V8	1970 6	1970 V8
Chevy 2												
Super Sport 2 dr	1737	1837	1737	1837	—	—	—	—	—	—	—	—
Chevelle 300												
2 dr sdn	3111	3211	3111	3211	3111	3211	3127	3227	—	—	—	—
4 dr sdn	3169	3269	3169	3269	3169	3269	—	—	—	—	—	—
2 dr sw 2 seat	3115	3215	—	—	—	—	—	—	—	—	—	—
300 Deluxe												
2 dr sdn	3311	3411	3311	3411	3311	3411	—	—	—	—	—	—
4 dr sdn	3369	3469	3369	3469	3369	3469	3369	3469	3369	3469	3369	3469
4 dr sw 2 seat	3335	3435	3335	3435	3335	3435	3335	3435	—	—	—	—
2 dr cpe	—	—	—	—	—	—	3327	3427	3327	3427	3327	3427
Sport cpe	—	—	—	—	—	—	3337	3437	3337	3437	3337	3437
Malibu												
Sport cpe	3537	3637	3517	3617	3517	3617	3537	3637	3537	3637	3537	3637
4 dr sdn	3569	3669	3569	3669	3569	3669	3569	3669	3569	3669	3569	3669
Sport 4 dr	—	—	3539	3639	3539	3639	3539	3639	3539	3639	3539	3639
Convrt	3567	3667	3567	3667	3567	3667	3567	3667	3567	3667	3567	3667
4 dr sw 2 seat	3535	3635	3535	3635	3535	3635	3535	3635	—	—	—	—
Malibu Super Sport												
Sport cpe	3737	3837	—	—	—	—	—	—	—	—	—	—
Convrt	3767	3867	—	—	—	—	—	—	—	—	—	—
SS 396												
2 dr cpe	—	—	—	3817	—	3817	—	3817	—	—	—	—
Convrt	—	—	—	3867	—	3867	—	3867	—	—	—	—
Biscayne												
2 dr sdn	5311	5411	5311	5411	5311	5411	5311	5411	5311	5411	5311	5411
4 dr sdn	5369	5469	5369	5469	5369	5469	5369	5469	5369	5469	5369	5469
4 dr sw 2 seat	5335	5435	5335	5435	5335	5435	5335	5435	—	—	—	—
Bel Air												
2 dr	5511	5611	5511	5611	5511	5611	5511	5611	5511	5611	5511	5611
4 dr sdn	5569	5669	5569	5669	5569	5669	5569	5669	5569	5669	5569	5669
4 dr sw 2 seat	5535	5635	5535	5635	5535	5635	5535	5635	—	—	—	—
4 dr sw 3 seat	5545	5645	5545	5645	5545	5645	5545	5645	—	—	—	—

	1965	1965	1966	1966	1967	1967	1968	1968	1968	1969	1969	1969
Impala												
Custom cpe	—	—	—	—	—	—	6347	6447	—	6447	—	—
Sport cpe	6337	6437	6337	6437	6387	6487	6387	6487	6337	6437	6337	6437
Sport sdn	6339	6439	6339	6439	6339	6439	6339	6439	6339	6439	6339	6439
4 dr sdn	6369	6469	6369	6469	6369	6469	6369	6469	6369	6469	6369	6469
Convrt	6367	6467	6367	6467	6367	6467	—	6467	—	6467	—	6467
4 dr sw 2 seat	6335	6435	6335	6435	6335	6435	—	6435	—	—	—	—
4 dr sw 3 seat	6345	6445	6345	6445	6345	6445	—	6445	—	—	—	—
Custom sport cpe	—	—	—	—	—	—	—	—	—	—	—	6447
Impala Super Sport												
Cpe	6537	6637	6737	6837	6787	6887	—	—	—	—	—	—
Convrt	6567	6667	6767	6867	6767	6867	—	—	—	—	—	—
Caprice												
2 dr	—	—	—	6647	—	6647	—	6647	—	6647	—	6647
4 dr	—	—	—	6639	—	6639	—	6639	—	6639	—	6639
4 dr sw 2 seat	—	—	—	6635	—	6635	—	6635	—	—	—	—
4 dr sw 3 seat	—	—	—	6645	—	6645	—	6645	—	—	—	—
Chevelle Nomad sw												
4 dr 2 seat	—	—	—	—	—	—	3135	3235	3135	3235	—	—
4 dr 3 seat Dual action Chevelle tail gate	—	—	—	—	—	—	—	—	3136	3236	3136	3236
Nomad sw Custom												
4 dr 2 seat	—	—	—	—	—	—	3335	3435	—	—	—	—
Chevelle Greenbrier sw												
4 dr 2 seat	—	—	—	—	—	—	—	—	3335	3435	—	—
4 dr 2 seat Dual action tail gate	—	—	—	—	—	—	—	—	3336	3436	3336	3436
4 dr 3 seat Dual action tail gate	—	—	—	—	—	—	—	—	—	—	—	3446

	1965	1965	1966	1966	1967	1967	1968	1968	1968	1969	1969	1969
Concours Stn Wgns												
4 dr 2 seat	—	—	—	—	3735	3835	3735	3835	—	—	—	—
4 dr 2 seat Dual action tail gate	—	—	—	—	—	—	—	—	3536	3636	3536	3636
4 dr 3 seat Dual action tail gate	—	—	—	—	—	—	—	—	3546	3646	—	3646
Estate Wgn 2 seat - Dual action tail gate	—	—	—	—	—	—	—	—	—	3836	—	3836
Estate wgn 3 seat - Dual action tail gate	—	—	—	—	—	—	—	—	—	3846	—	3846
Monte Carlo												
2 dr	—	—	—	—	—	—	—	—	—	—	—	3857
4 dr	—	—	—	—	—	—	—	—	—	—	—	3867
El Camino 300	—	—	3380	3480	3380	3480	3380	3480	3380	3480	3380	3480
El Camino Custm	—	—	3580	3680	3580	3680	3580	3680	3580	3680	3580	3680
Brookwood Sw												
4 dr 2 seat Dual action tail gate	—	—	—	—	—	—	—	—	5336	5436	—	5436
Townsman sw												
4 dr 2 seat Dual action tail gate	—	—	—	—	—	—	—	—	5536	5636	—	5636
4 dr 3 seat Dual action tail gate	—	—	—	—	—	—	—	—	5546	5646	—	5646
Kingswood sw												
4 dr 2 seat Dual action tail gate	—	—	—	—	—	—	—	—	—	6436	—	6436
4 dr 3 seat Dual action tail gate	—	—	—	—	—	—	—	—	—	6446	—	6446
Estate Wagon												
2 seat - Dual Action tail gate	—	—	—	—	—	—	—	—	—	6636	—	6636
Estate wagon 3 seat - Dual action tail gate	—	—	—	—	—	—	—	—	—	6646	—	6646

	1965	1965	1966	1966	1967	1967	1968	1968	1968	1969	1969	1969
Corvette Stingray												
Cpe	—	9437	—	9437	—	9437	—	9437	—	9437	—	9437
Convrt	—	9467	—	9467	—	9467	—	9467	—	9467	—	9467
Camero												
Cpe	—	—	—	—	2337	2437	2337	2437	2337	2437	2387	2487
Convrt	—	—	—	—	2367	2467	2367	2467	2367	2467	—	—

The sixth number designates the year model.

5	1965		8	1968	1	1971
6	1966		9	1969		
7	1967		0	1970		

The seventh letter designates the assembly plant.

The last six numbers are the sequential production numbers.

CHRYSLER

1955 to 1965. V.I.N. plate is spot welded to the left front door hinge post. (Illus. 32)

1959. Some models have the V.I.N. plate located on the top left side of the cowl under the hood. (Illus. 48 at B)

1966 and 1967. V.I.N. plate is riveted to the left front door hinge post. (Illus. 32)

1968 to 1971. V.I.N. plate is located on the left side of the dashboard visible through the windshield. (Illus. 33 at B)

Assembly plants, their symbol designator and location.

3   Jefferson, Mich   1966
3   Detroit, Mich   1960 to 1965 and 1967
5   Los Angeles, Calif   1960 only
6   Newark, N.J.   1966
6   Delaware   1965 and 1967
C   Detroit, Mich   1968 to 1970
F   Newark, Del   1968 to 1970

1960 to 1965.

Sample V.I.N. plate with number:

```
┌─────────────────────────────┐
│         VEHICLE NO.         │
│          C156123456         │
└─────────────────────────────┘
```

First number (letter for the 1965 model) designates the Chrysler automobile.

8   1960 to 1964. Chrysler division of Chrysler Corporation.
C   1965. Chrysler division of Chrysler Corporation.

Second number designates the series.

1   1960 Windsor
       1961 to 1965 Newport
2   1960 Saratoga
       1961 Windsor
       1962 to 1965 300 series

Second number designates the series.
3   1960 to 1965 New Yorker
4   1960 to 1965 300F, 300G, 300H, 300J, 300K, 300L.
5   1960 Windsor station wagon
    1961 to 1965 Newport station wagon
7   1960 to 1965 New Yorker station wagon
8   1964 New Yorker Salon
9   1965 Police Special

Third number designates the year model.

0	1960	2	1962	4	1964
1	1961	3	1963	5	1965

Fourth number designates the assembly plant.
The last six numbers are the sequential production numbers.

1966.

Sample V.I.N. plate with number:
Same as 1965

First letteer designates the Chrysler automobile.
C   Chrysler Division of Chrysler Corporation.

Second letter designates the series model.
L   Newport
L   Town and Country station wagon
H   New Yorker
M   300 series

Third and fourth numbers designate the body style.
23 Newport 2 dr ht
    300 2 dr ht
    New Yorker 2 dr ht
27 Newport convertible
    300 convertible
41 Newport 4 dr sdn
42 Newport town 4 dr sdn
    New Yorker town 4 dr sdn
43 Newport 4 dr ht
    300 4 dr ht
    New Yorker 4 dr ht
45 Town and Country 2 seat station wagon
46 Town and Country 3 seat station wagon

Fourth letter designates the engine type.
G   383-2V   V8
G   383-4V   V8
J   440-4V   V8

Sixth number designates the year model.
6   1966

Seventh number designates the assembly plant.

The last six numbers are the sequential production numbers.

1967 to 1971.

Sample V.I.N. with number:

CL27H0F123456

First letter designates Chrysler automobile.

C   Chrysler division of Chrysler Corporation.

Second letter designates the body series.

E   1967 to 1970 Newport
     1967 to 1969 Town and Country station wagon
H   1967 to 1970 New Yorker
L   1967 to 1970 Newport Custom
M   1967 to 1970 300 series
P   1970 Town and Country station wagon

Third and fourth numbers designate the body style.

23   New Yorker H T Cpe
     Newport and Newport Custom H T Cpe
27   Newport convertible
     300 convertible
41   New Yorker 4 dr sdn
     Newport 4 dr sdn
43   New Yorker 4 dr ht sdn
     Newport 4 dr ht sdn
     300 4 dr ht sd n
45   Town and Country station wagon 2 seat
46   Town and Country station wagon 3 seat

Fifth letter designates the engine type.

G   383-2V   V8   1967 to 1969
H   383-4V   V8   1967 to 1969
K   440-2V   V8   1967 to 1969
L   440-4V   V8   1967 to 1969
L   383-2V   V8   1970
T   440-2V   V8   1970

Sixth number designates the year model.

7   1967   9   1969   1   1971
8   1968   0   1970

Seventh letter designates the assembly plant.

The last six numbers are the sequential production numbers.

DODGE

1955 to 1964. V.I.N. plate is spot welded to the left front door hinge post. (Illus. 32)

1959. V.I.N. plate may be found on the left side of the cowl under the hood. (Illus. 48 at B)

1965 to 1967. V.I.N. plate is riveted to the left front door hinge post. (Illus. 32)

1968 to 1971. V.I.N. plate is located on the left side of the dashboard visible through the windshield. (Illus. 33 at B)

1	Detroit, Mich (Plymouth) 1963 to 1965
1	Lynch Road, Mo 1966
2	Detroit, Mich (Dodge) 1960 to 1965
2	Hamtramck, Mich 1966
3	Detroit, Mich (Jefferson) 1960 to 1962
3	Detroit, Mich 1966
3	Jefferson, Mich 1963 to 1965
4	Belvedere, Ill. 1966
5	Los Angeles, Calif 1960 to 1966, 1968 to 1970
6	Newark, Del 1960 to 1966
7	St. Louis, Mo 1960 to 1966, 1968 to 1970
8	Clairpoint 1960
9	Windsor, Ontario, Canada 1968 to 1970
A	Lynch Road, Mo 1968 to 1970
B	Hamtramch, Mich 1968 to 1970
C	Detroit, Mich 1969 to 1970
D	Belvedere, Ill 1968 to 1970
E	Los Angeles, Calif 1968 to 1970
F	Newark, Del 1968 to 1970
H	New Stanton 1970
P	Wyoming 1969
R	Windsor, Ontario, Canada 1968 to 1970

1960

Sample V.I.N. plate with number

```
VEHICLE NO.
51051234SC
```

First number designates the series make.

4	Dart 6 Cyl Seneca, Pioneer, Phoenix
5	Dart V8 Seneca, Pioneer, Phoenix
6	Matador V8
6	Polara V8

Second number designates the series model.

1	Seneca	5	Seneca Station Wagon
1	Matador	5	Matador Station Wagon
2	Pioneer	6	Pioneer Station Wagon
3	Phoenix	7	Polara Station Wagon
3	Polara		

Third number designates the year model.

0   1960

Fourth number designates the assembly plant.

The last six numbers are the sequential production numbers.

1961

V.I.N. same as 1960

First number designates the engine type.

4   Dart 6 Cyl
     Seneca 6 Cyl
     Pioneer 6 Cyl
     Phoenix 6 Cyl
5   Polara V8
7   Lancer 6 Cyl

Second number designates series model.

1   Seneca
1   Lancer
2   Pioneeer
3   Phoenix
3   Lancer
4   Polara
5   Seneca and Lancer Station Wagon
6   Pioneer Station Wagon
7   Polara and Lancer Station Wagon
8   Taxi

Third number designates the year.

1   1961

Fourth number designates the assembly plant.

The last 6 numbers are the sequential production numbers.

1962

V.I.N. same as 1960 to 1961.

First and second numbers designate the body series and type.

40   Dart Sedan 6 Cyl
41   Dart Sedan 6 Cyl
42   Dart 300, Sedan and Coupe 6 Cyl
43   Dart 400, Sedan and Coupe 6 Cyl
45   Dart Station Wagon 6 Cyl
46   Dart 300, Station Wagon 6 Cyl
48   Dart Taxi 6 Cyl
50   Dart Sedan V8
51   Dart Sedan V8
52   Dart 300, Sedan and Coupe V8
53   Dart 400, Sedan and Coupe V8
54   Polara 500 all V8

First and second numbers designate the body series and type.
55 Dart Station Wagon V8
56 Dart 300 Station Wagon V8
57 Dart 400 Station Wagon V8
58 Dart Taxi V8
61 Custom 880 Sedan and Convertible V8
65 Custom 880 Station Wagon V8
71 Lancer 170 Sedan 6 Cyl
73 Lancer 770 Sedan 6 Cyl
74 Lancer GT Coupe 6 Cyl
75 Lancer 170 Station Wagon 6 Cyl
77 Lancer 770 Station Wagon 6 Cyl
78 Lancer Taxi 6 Cyl

Third number designates the year model.
2   1962

Fourth number designates the assembly plant.

The last six numbers are the sequential production numbers.

1963 to 1965
V.I.N. same as 1959 to 1962.

First number or letter designates the series model.
2   1965 Dart 6 Cyl
4   1965 Coronet 6 Cyl
4   1964 and 1963 Dodge 6 Cyl
5   1964 and 1963 880 Series
6   1963 and 1964 Dodge V8
7   1963 and 1964 Dart 6 Cyl
D   1965 880 Series Polar Series, Monaco Series
L   1965 Dart V8
W   1965 Coronet V8

Second number designates the body type.

DART
1   1963, 1964, 1965 Dart 170
3   1963, 1964, 1965 Dart 270
4   1963, 1964, 1965 Dart GT
5   1963, 1964, 1965 Dart 170 Station Wagon
7   1963, 1964, 1965 Dart 270 Station Wagon

DODGE
1   1963, 1964, 1965 330, 880, 330 Custom, 880 Custom, Coronet, Polara
2   1963, 1964, 440 Custom, 880 Custom
3   1963, 1964, 1965 Polara, Custom 880, Coronet 440
4   1963, 1964, 1965 Polara 500, Polara Sport Package, Monaco, Coronet 500
5   1963, 1964, 1965 330 Station Wagon, 880 Station Wagon, Coronet Station Wagon
6   1963 to 1964 440 Station Wagon, 880 Custom Station Wagon

Second number designates the body type.
7   1965 Coronet 440 Station Wagon, Custom 880 Station Wagon, 1963 Polara Station Wagon
8   1963, 1964, 1965 Taxi
9   1963, 1964, 1965 Police
0   1963 Fleet 880

Third number designates the year model.
3   1963
4   1964
5   1965

Fourth number designates the assembly plant.

The last 6 numbers are the sequential production number.

1966 to 1971
Sample V.I.N. plate and number.

DL43F9A123456

First letter designates names of model.
D   Dodge, Polara, Monaco
J   Challenger
L   Dart
W   Coronet
A   Charger

Second letter designates the name of the series.
E   1966 Polara 318 and 1966 and 1967 Coronet
L   1966 to 1970 Dart, Coronet Deluxe, Polara, Dart Swinger
H   1966 to 1970 Dart 270, Dart Custom, Monaco, Coronet 440, Charger, Challenger, Dart Swinger
     1968 Coronet
P   1966 to 1968 Monaco 550, Charger, Coronet 500, Dart GT
     1969 Dart GT, Coronet 500, Charger
     1970 Charger 500, Coronet 500
M   1966 to 1969 Polara 500, Super Bee
M   1970 Super Bee Swinger 340
S   1970 Coronet RT, Charger RT, Challenger RT
     1968 to 1969 Dart GTS, Coronet RT, Charger RT
X   1969 Charger 500
N   1969 Coronet New York Taxi
T   1968 to 1969 Dodge and Coronet Taxi
K   1966 to 1969 Police Dodge and Coronet

Third and Fourth numbers designate body series.
21   2 Dr Sedan
     1969 to 1970 Coronet Super Bee, 2 Door Sedan
     1966 to 1970 Coronet Deluxe
     1966 & 1968 Coronet
     1966 Dart Custom
     1966 to 1968 Dart
     1967, 1969, 1970 Coronet 440

Third and fourth numbers designate the body series.
23   HT Coupes
     1966 to 1970 Dart GT, Dart Custom
     1969 & 1970 Dart Swinger
     1969 Dart
     1969 & 1970 Coronet Super Bee
     1969 Dart GT Sport
     1967 to 1970 Coronet RT
     1966 to 1970 Coronet 500
     1966, 1968 to 1970 Coronet 440
     1966 to 1968 Monaco 500
     1966 to 1970 Monaco and Polara
     1967 to 1969 Polara 500
     1970 Challenger & CRT
27   Convertibles
     1966 to 1969 Dart GT
     1966 Dart Custom
     1969 Dart GT Sport
     1967 to 1970 Coronet RT
     1966 to 1970 Coronet 500
     1966 & 1967 Coronet 440
     1967 to 1969 Polara 500
     1966 to 1970 Polara
     1970 Challenger & CRT
29   Sport Coupe
     1969 to 1970 Charger 500 & RT
     1966 to 1970 Charger
     1970 Challenger & CRT
41   4 Dr Sedan
     1966 to 1970 Dart Custom & Dart, Coronet Deluxe, Coronet 440 &
     Coronet 550, Polara & Monaco
     1966 & 1968 Coronet
     1966 & 1967 Polara 318
43   HT 4 Dr Sedan
     1966 to 1970 Monaco, Polara
45   2 Seat Station Wagon
     1966 to 1970 Monaco, Polara, Coronet Deluxe, Coronet 440
     1966 Dart Custom & Dart
     1967 Coronet
     1968 to 1970 Coronet 550
46   3 Seat Station Wagon
     1966 to 1970 Monaco, Polara, Coronet 440
     1968 to 1970 Coronet 550

Fifth letter designates the engine type.
A   6 Cyl 170   1966 to 1969
B   6 Cyl 198   1970
B   6 Cyl 225   1966 to 1969
C   6 Cyl 225   1970
C   6 Cyl Special   1966 to 1969
D   V8 273   1966 to 1969

Fifth letter designates the engine type.

E	6 Cyl Special	1970
E	V8 Hi Perf	1967 & 1968
E	V8 318	1966
F	V8 318	1967 to 1969
F	V8 361	1966
G	V8 318	1970
G	V8 383	1966 to 1969
H	V8 383 Hi Perf	1967 to 1969
H	V8 426	1966
H	V8 340 Hi Perf	1970
J	V8 426	1967 to 1969
J	V8 440	1966
K	V8 440	1967 to 1969
K	V8 Special	1966
L	V8 383	1970
L	V8 440 Hi Perf	1967 to 1969
M	V8 Special	1967 to 1969
N	V8 383 Hi Perf	1970
N	V8 340	1968
P	V8 340 Hi Perf	1968 to 1969
R	V8 426	1970
T	V8 440	1970
U	V8 440 Hi Perf	1970
V	V8 440	3/2 Brl Carbs
Z	V8 Special 1970	

Sixth number designates the year model.

6	1966	8	1968	0	1970
7	1967	9	1969		

Seventh letter or number designates the assembly plant.

The last six numbers are the sequential production numbers.

Illus. 53

Warranty plate found on Ford, Mercury and Lincoln autos. They should NOT be confused with vehicle identification number.

FORD

Ford Motor Company automobiles (Ford, Mercury and Lincoln) has what resembles a vehicle identification plate riveted to the left front door hinge post or to the outer face of the left front door. (Illus. 53) of 1955 to 1967 automobiles. These are warranty plates. They are NOT to be used for identifying these vehicles as the number on these plates may not be the same as the vehicle identification number. A damaged door can be replaced with one purchased from a wrecking yard, thus reflecting an incorrect number.

1955 to 1962. Ford and Mercury standard size autos and 1955 to 1958 Lincolns. V.I.N. is stamped on top of the right frame rail in the area between forward of the firewall to opposite the radiator saddle.

1963 to 1967 Ford and Mercury and 1967 Thunderbird. V.I.N. is stamped on a metal extension of the firewall, top of right side, under the hood. (Illus. 48 at G)

1958 to 1960 Lincoln. V.I.N. is stamped into body panel near the trunk latch.

1961 to 1967 Lincoln. V.I.N. is stamped into the right front inner fender panel over or near the "A" frame opening.

1960 to 1963 Comet, Falcon, Ranchero. V.I.N. is stamped into the left support brace, extending from the firewall to the shock absorber housing, under the hood. (Illus. 48 at C)

1959 and 1960 Thunderbird. V.I.N. is stamped on top of the right front spring housing under the hood.

1961 to 1966 Thunderbird. V.I.N. is stamped into the body panel to right of the hood latch.

1962 to 1965 Comet, Fairlane, Falcon, Meteor, and Ranchero.

1965 to 1967 Comet, Couger, and Mustang. V.I.N. is stamped into left front inner fender panel at top under the hood. (Illus. 48 at D or E)

1966 and 1967 Comet, Falcon, and Fairlane. V.I.N. is stamped into top left of the radiator support bar under the hood. (Illus. 48 at F)

1968 all Ford Motor Company automobiles. V.I.N. plate is located on the right side of the dashboard visible through the windshield. (Illus. 33 at A)

1969 to 1971 all Ford Motor Company automobiles. V.I.N. plate is located on the left side of the dashboard visible through the windshield. (Illus. 33 at B)

Assembly plants, their symbol designator and location.

A	Atlanta, Ga.	1960 to 1966
B	Oakville, Ontario, Canada	1967 to 1971
C	Chester, Pa.	1960 to 1962
D	Dallas, Tex.	1960 to 1966
E	Mahwah, N.J.	1960 to 1966
F	Dearborn, Mich.	1960 to 1971
G	Chicago, Ill.	1960 to 1966
H	Lorain, Ohio	1960 to 1971
J	Los Angeles, Calif.	1960 to 1967
K	Kansas City, Mo.	1960 to 1966
L	Michigan Truck Assembly	1965 and 1966
N	Norfolk, Va.	1960 to 1966
P	Twin Cities, Minn.	1960 to 1966
R	San Jose, Calif.	1960 to 1971
S	Pilot Plant, Mich.	1960 to 1971
T	Metuchen, N.J.	1960 to 1966
U	Louisville, Ky.	1960 to 1966
W	Wayne, Mich.	1962 to 1967
Y	Wixom, Mich.	1960 to 1966 and 1968
Z	St. Louis, Mo.	1961 to 1971

1960 to 1970.
Sample V.I.N.

OH38V123456

First number designates the year model.

0	1960	4	1964	8	1968
1	1961	5	1965	9	1969
2	1962	6	1966	0	1970
3	1963	7	1967	1	1971

Second letter designates the assembly plant.

Third and fourth numbers designate the series model.

Falcon Series	Body Style	Year
01	2 dr cpe	1966
02	4 dr sdn	1966
06	4 dr stn wgn	1966
10	2 dr cpe	1967 to 1970
11	4 dr sdn	1967 to 1970
11	Futura clb cpe	1966
11	Futura Sport cpe	1966
12	Futura 4 dr sdn	1966
12	4 dr stn wgn	1967 to 1970
16	4 dr stn wgn	1966
20	Futura 2 dr cpe	1967
20	Futura 2 dr cpe	1968 to 1970
21	Futura 4 dr sdn	1967 to 1970
22	Futura Sport cpe	1967 to 1969
23	Futura 4 dr stn wgn	1967 to 1970
27	Ranchero	1966

Mustang	Body Style	Year
01	HT Cpe	1967 to 1970
02	Fastback cpe	1967 to 1970
03	Convert	1967 to 1970
05	Mach I	1970
04	Grande	1970
07	HT Cpe	1966
07	Convert	1966
09	Fastback cpe	1966

Fairlane	Body Style	Year
30	2 dr ht	1968 and 1969
30	2 dr sdn	1967
31	2 dr sdn	1966
31	4 dr sdn	1967 to 1969
32	4 dr sdn	1966

Fairlane 500	Body Style	Year
28	4 dr sdn	1970
33	2 dr sdn	1967
33	2 dr ht	1968 and 1969
34	4 dr sdn	1967 to 1969
35	Fastback cpe	1968 and 1969
35	2 dr ht	1967
36	Convert	1967 to 1969
41	2 dr sdn	1966
42	4 dr sdn	1966
43	2 dr ht	1966
45	Convert	1966
70	2 dr sdn	1969

Third and fourth numbers designate the series model.

Fairlane Torino

30	2 dr ht	1970
31	4 dr sdn	1970
32	4 dr ht sdn	1970
33	2 dr ht Brougham	1970
35	2 dr ht cpe GT	1970
36	4 dr ht sdn Brougham	1970
37	Convert	1970
40	2 dr ht	1968 and 1969
41	4 dr sdn	1968 and 1969
42	4 dr ht cpe GT	1968 and 1969
43	Convert	1968 and 1969
44	2 dr ht	1968 and 1969

Fairlane Cobra

38	2 dr ht fastback	1970
45	2 dr ht	1969
46	2 dr ht fastback	1969

Fairlane 500 XL

40	2 dr ht	1967
41	Convert	1967
46	2 dr ht	1966
47	Convert	1966

Fairlane GT and GTA

40	2 dr ht	1966
42	2 dr ht	1967
43	Convert	1967
44	Convert	1966

Fairlane Station Wagons

32	4 dr sw	1967 to 1969
37	4 dr sw 500	1967 to 1969
38	4 dr Ranch wgn	1966
38	4 dr Squire	1967
38	Torino Squire	1968 and 1969
41	4 dr sw 500	1970
42	Torino sw	1970
43	Torino Squire sw	1970
48	Custom Ranch Wgn	1966
49	Squire 4 dr sw	1966

Ranchero

46	Ranchero	1970
47	Ranchero	1967 to 1969
47	Ranchero 500	1970
48	Ranchero 500	1967 to 1969
48	Ranchero 500 GT	1970
49	Ranchero 500 XL	1967
49	Ranchero Squire	1970

Third and fourth numbers designate the series model.

Ford Custom

50	2 dr sdn	1967 to 1969
51	4 dr sdn	1967 to 1970
53	2 dr sdn	1966
54	4 dr sdn	1966

Ford Custom 500

51	2 dr sdn	1966
52	2 dr sdn	1967 to 1969
52	4 dr sdn	1966
53	4 dr sdn	1967 to 1970
59	2 dr ht	1970

Ford Galaxie 500

54	4 dr sdn	1967 to 1970
55	2 dr ht Fastback	1968 to 1970
55	2 dr ht	1967
56	4 dr ht	1967 to 1970
57	Convert	1967 to 1969
58	2 dr ht	1968 to 1970
62	4 dr sdn	1966
64	4 dr ht	1966
65	Convert	1965
66	2 dr ht	1966

Ford Galaxie 500 XL

60	2 dr ht	1968 and 1969
61	Convert	1968 and 1969
68	2 dr ht	1966 and 1967
69	Convert	1966 and 1967

Ford LTD

62	2 dr ht	1970
66	4 dr ht	1970
64	4 dr sdn	1970

Ford Galaxie 500 LTD

60	4 dr ht	1966
62	2 dr ht	1968 and 1969
64	4 dr sdn	1968 and 1969
66	4 dr ht	1968 and 1969
67	2 dr ht	1966

Ford Galaxie 500 7.0 Litre

61	2 dr ht	1966
63	Convert	1966

Third and fourth numbers designate the series model.

Station Wagons

70	Ranch Wagon 4 dr 2 seat	1967 to 1970
71	Country Sedan 4 dr 2 seat	1967
71	Ranch Wagon 4 dr 2 seat	1966
72	Country Sedan 4 dr 2 seat	1966
72	Country Sedan 4 dr 3 seat	1967
73	Country Sedan 4 dr 2 seat	1968 to 1970
73	Country Squire 4 dr 2 seat	1967
74	Country Sedan 4 dr 3 seat	1966, 1968 to 1970
74	Country Squire 4 dr 3 seat	1967
75	Country Squire 4 dr 2 seat	1968 to1970
76	Country Squire 4 dr 3 seat	1966
76	Country Squire 4 dr 3 seat	1968 to 1970
78	Country Squire 4 dr 3 seat	1966

Ford Custom 500 Station Wagons

71	Ranch Wagon 4 dr 2 seat	1968 to 1970
72	Ranch Wagon 4 dr 3 seat	1968 to 1970

Thunderbird

81	Town 2 dr ht	1966
81	2 dr ht	1967
82	2 dr ht Landau	1967
83	2 dr ht	1966, 1968 to 1970
84	4 dr sdn	1967
84	2 dr ht Landau	1968 to 1970
85	Convert	1966
86	4 dr town sdn	1968
87	2 dr ht town Landau	1966
87	4 dr sdn Landau	1968 to 1970

Fifth letter or number designates the engine type.

U	170-1V	6 Cyl	1966 to 1970
T	200-IV	6 Cyl	1966 to 1970
S	200-1V	6 Cyl	1966
V	240-1V	6 Cyl	1966 to 1970
E	240-1V	6 Cyl	1966 to 1970 Taxi Special
J	240-1V	6 Cyl	1966 Low compression
5	240-1V	6 Cyl	1970 Low compression
B	240-IV	6 Cyl	1966 to 1970 Police special
2	200-IV	6 Cyl	1966 to 1967 Export model
2	200-1V	6 Cyl	1969 and 1970
L	250-1V	6 Cyl	1969 and 1970
3	250-1V	6 Cyl	1970 Low compression
C	289-2V	V8	1966 to 1968
A	289-4V	V8	1966 and 1967
K	289-4V	V8	1966 High performance
F	302-2V	V8	1968 to 1970
6	302-2V	V8	1968 to 1970 Low compression
D	302-2V	V8	1969 and 1970 Police and Taxi special
J	302-4V	V8	1968 High output
G	302-4V	V8	1970 High output
H	351-2V	V8	1969 and 1970
M	351-4V	V8	1969 and 1970
X	352-4V	V8	1966
Y	390-2V	V8	1966 to 1970 Regular fuel
X	390-2V	V8	1968 and 1970 Premium fuel
H	390-2V	V8	1966 and 1967
Z	390-4V	V8	1966 to 1968
S	390-4V	V8	1967 to 1970
P	390-4V	V8	1966 Police special
M	410-4V	V8	1966
W	427-4V	V8	1966 to 1969
R	427-8V	V8	1966 and 1967
L	427-4V	V8	1967 Over head cam
D	427-8V	V8	1967 Over head cam
Q	428-4V	V8	1966 to 1970 Cobra Jet
P	428-4V	V8	1966 to 1970 Police special
3	289-2V	V8	1967 Export model
8	428-4V	V8	1967 Export model
8	428-4V	V8	1968 Low compression
R	428-4V	V8	1969 and 1970 Cobra Jet Ram Air
K	429-2V	V8	1969 and 1970
N	429-4V	V8	1968 to 1970
C	429-4V	V8	1970 Cobra Jet
J	429-4V	V8	1970 Cobra Jet Ram Air
Z	429-4V	V8	1970 High output

The last six numbers are the sequential production numbers.

JEEP

1960 to 1971. V.I.N. plate located on either the left or right side of the firewall under the hood.

1965 to 1971. Jeep passenger vehicle and pickup. V.I.N. plate is screwed to the left front door hinge post. The six sequential production numbers of the V.I.N. are also stamped on the top right frame rail between the shock absorber and the radiator.

LINCOLN

1960 to 1971.

Sample V.I.N. (Note asterisks 1960 to 1967)

4Y82N123456

1968 to 1971:   9S89A123456

First number designates the year model.

0	1960	3	1963	6	1966	9	1969
1	1961	4	1964	7	1967	0	1970
2	1962	5	1965	8	1968	1	1971

Second letter designates the assembly plant.

S   Pilot Plant, Mich.   1964 to 1970
Y   Wixom, Mich.   1960 to 1970

Third and forth numbers designate the body series.

62   1960 Lincoln 4 dr sdn
63   1960 Lincoln 2 dr ht
64   1960 Lincoln 4 dr ht
72   1960 Lincoln Premier 4 dr sdn
73   1960 Lincoln Premier 2 dr ht
74   1960 Lincoln Premier 4 dr ht
81   1968 to 1970 Lincoln Continental 2 dr ht
82   1960 to 1970 Lincoln Continental 4 dr sdn
83   1960 Lincoln Continental 2 dr ht
84   1960 Lincoln Continental 4 dr ht
85   1960 Lincoln Continental 2 dr convert
86   1961 to 1967 Lincoln Continental 4 dr convert
89   1966 and 1967 Lincoln Continental 2 dr ht
89   1968 to 1970 Mark III 2 dr ht
92   1960 Lincoln town car
99   1960 Lincoln limousine

Fifth letter or number designates the engine type.

A   460-4V   V8   1968 to 1970
G   462-4V   V8   1966 to 1968
H   430-4V   V8   1960 to 1963
N   430-4V   V8   1964 and 1965
1   460-4V   V8   1968
7   462-4V   V8   1966 and 1967 Export model
7   462-4V   V8   1968 low compression

The last six numbers are the sequential production numbers.

MERCURY

1960 to 1971.

Sample V.I.N. (Note asterisks 1960 to 1967)

4E34T123456

1968 to 1971	9H44S123456

First number designates the year model.

0	1960	4	1964	8	1968
1	1961	5	1965	9	1969
2	1962	6	1966	0	1970
3	1963	7	1967	1	1971

Second letter designates the assembly plant.

B	Oakville, Onterio, Canada 1967 to 1970
E	Manwak, N.J. 1961 to 1963
F	Dearborn, Mich. 1962 to 1970
H	Lorain, Ohio 1960 to 1970
J	Los Angeles, Calif. 1960 to 1967
K	Kansas City, Mo. 1960 to 1964
R	San Jose, Calif. 1960 to 1964, 1968 to 1970
S	Pilot Plant, Mich. 1960 to 1970
T	Metuchen, N.J. 1960, 1962 to 1966
W	Wayne, Mich. 1960 to 1967
Y	Wixom, Mich. 1968

Third and forth numbers designate the body series.

Comet 202

01	2 dr sdn	1960, 1963 to 1968
02	4 dr sdn	1960, 1963 to 1967
06	2 dr sw	1960
07	4 dr sw	1960
21	2 dr sw	1963
32	4 dr sw	1963 to 1965

Comet 404

11	2 dr sdn	1961 to 1965
12	4 dr sdn	1961 to 1965
15	Convert	1963
21	2 dr sw	1961 to 1963
22	4 dr sw	1961
23	2 dr sw	1962 and 1963
24	4 dr sw	1962 and 1963
34	4 dr sw	1964 and 1965
36	Woodside sw	1964 and 1965

Comet Capri

06	4 dr sdn	1967
07	2 dr ht	1967
12	4 dr sdn	1966
13	2 dr ht	1966

Third and fourth numbers designate the body series.

Comet Caliente

10	4 dr sdn	1967
11	2 dr ht	1967
12	Convert	1967
22	4 dr sdn	1964 to 1966
23	2 dr ht	1964 to 1966
25	Convert	1964 to 1966

Comet Cyclone

15	2 dr ht	1967
16	Convert	1967
17	S22 2 dr ht	1962
18	S22 Convert	1963
19	S22 4 dr sdn	1963
26	GT 2 dr ht	1966
27	2 dr ht	1964 to 1966
28	GT Convert	1966
29	Convert	1966

Comet Station Wagons

03	4 dr Voyager	1967
06	4 dr Voyager	1966
08	4 dr Villager	1967
16	4 dr Villager	1966
26	4 dr Villager	1963

Meteor

31	2 dr sdn	1962 and 1963
32	4 dr sdn	1962 and 1963
38	4 dr sw	1963
41	2 dr sdn	1961
42	4 dr sdn	1961

Meteor Custom

41	2 dr sdn	1962 and 1963
42	4 dr sdn	1962 and 1963
43	2 dr ht	1963
47	S33 2 dr ht	1963
47	4 dr sw	1963
49	Country Crusier sw	1963
51	2 dr sdn	1961
52	4 dr sdn	1961
54	4 dr ht	1961
57	2 dr ht	1961

Mercury Monterey

31	2 dr sdn	1960
32	4 dr sdn	1960
33	2 dr ht	1960
34	4 dr ht	1969
35	Convert	1960
41	2 dr sdn	1964

Third and fourth numbers designate the body series.

42	4 dr sdn	1964 to 1966
43	2 dr ht	1964
43	2 dr sdn	1965 and 1966
44	4 dr sdn	1966
44	4 dr ht	1969
44	2 dr sdn	1970
45	Convert	1964 to 1970
46	2 dr ht	1969 and 1970
47	2 dr ht fastback	1964 and 1965
47	2 dr ht	1966 to 1968
48	4 dr ht	1968 to 1970
48	4 dr ht fastback	1964 to 1967
51	2 dr sdn	1962 and 1963
52	4 dr sdn	1962 and 1963
53	2 dr ht	1962 and 1963
54	4 dr ht	1962 and 1963
72	4 dr sw	1969 and 1970

Mercury Custom

37	Commuter sw	1960
45	S55 Convert	1967
47	S55 2 dr ht	1967
54	4 dr sdn	1969 and 1970
56	2 dr ht	1969 and 1970
57	Colony Park sw	1960
58	4 dr ht	1969 and 1970
62	4 dr sdn	1961 to 1963
63	2 dr ht	1962 and 1963
64	4 dr ht	1961 to 1963
65	Convert	1961 to 1963
67	2 dr ht	1961
67	S55 2 dr ht	1963
69	S55 Convert	1963
72	Commuter SW	1962, 1964 to 1966
74	Commuter sw	1961 and 1969
76	Colony Park sw	1961 to 1966

Mercury Montclair

42	4 dr sdn	1960
43	2 dr ht	1960
44	4 dr ht fastback	1960
52	4 dr sdn	1964 and 1965
53	2 dr ht	1965
54	4 dr sdn	1966 to 1968
57	2 dr ht fastback	1964 to 1968
58	4 dr ht fastback	1965 and 1968

Mercury Parklane

53	2 dr ht	1960
54	4 dr ht	1960
55	Convert	1960

Third and fourth numbers designate the body series.

62	4 dr sdn	1964 to 1966
63	2 dr ht	1964
64	4 dr ht	1964, 1967 and 1968
65	Convert	1964 to 1968
67	2 dr ht fastback	1964 to 1968
68	4 dr ht fastback	1964 to 1968

Montego

01	Sport Coupe	1969 and 1970
02	Sport Sedan	1969 and 1970
03	Stn Wgn	1968 and 1969
06	4 dr sdn	1968 and 1969
07	2 dr ht	1968 and 1969

Montego MX

06	4 dr sdn	1970
07	2 dr ht	1970
08	Stn Wgn	1968 to 1970
10	4 dr sdn	1968 and 1969
11	2 dr ht	1968 and 1969
12	Convert	1968 and 1969

Montego MX Brougham

10	4 dr sdn	1968 to 1970
11	2 dr ht	1968 to 1970
12	4 dr ht	1970

Montego Cyclone

15	2 dr ht	1970
15	2 dr ht fastback	1968 and 1969
16	2 dr ht GT	1970
16	2 dr ht fastback	1969
17	2 dr ht	1968
17	2 dr ht Spoiler	1970

Couger

91	2 dr ht	1967 to 1970
92	Convert	1969 and 1970
93	2 dr ht	1968

Couger XR 7

93	2 dr ht	1969 and 1970
94	Convert	1969 and 1970

Mercury Marauder

60	2 dr ht	1969
60	2 dr ht tunnel roof	1970
61	2 dr ht X100	1969
61	2 dr ht X100 tunnel roof	1970

Parklane Brougham

64	4 dr sdn	1968
68	4 dr ht	1968

Third and fourth numbers designate the body series.

Mercury Brougham

61	4 dr sdn	1967
62	4 dr ht	1967

Marquis

40	4 dr ht	1969 and 1970
41	2 dr ht	1969 and 1970
42	4 dr ht	1969 and 1970
62	4 dr ht	1970
63	4 dr ht	1969 and 1970
64	2 dr ht	1970
65	Convert	1969 and 1970
66	2 dr ht	1969 and 1970
67	4 dr ht	1970
68	4 dr ht	1969 and 1970
69	2 dr ht	1967 and 1968
74	Stn Wgn	1970
76	Colony Park	1969 and 1970

Fifth letter or number designates the engine type.

S	144-1V	6 Cyl	1960 to 1963
U	170-1V	6 Cyl	1961 to 1964 and 1966
T	200-1V	6 Cyl	1964 to 1968
2	200-IV	6 Cyl	1967 Export Model
V	223-1V	6 Cyl	1961 and 1962
V	240-1V	6 Cyl	1966
B	240-1V	6 Cyl	1966 Police Special
E	240-1V	6 Cyl	1966 Taxi Model
L	250-IV	6 Cyl	1969 and 1970
3	250-1V	6 Cyl	1969 and 1970
L	221-2V	V8	1962 and 1963
F	260-2V	V8	1962 to 1964
C	289-2V	V8	1965 and 1967
3	289-2V	V8	1967 Export model
A	289-4V	V8	1965 and 1967
K	289-4V	V8	1964 and 1966
W	292-2V	V8	1961 and 1962
F	302-2V	V8	1968 to 1970
6	302-2V	V8	1968 to 1970
J	302-4V	V8	1968
G	302-2V	V8	1970 High Output
P	312-2V	V8	1960
H	351-2V	V8	1969 and 1970
M	351-4V	V8	1969 and 1970
X	352-2V	V8	1961 and 1962
X	352-4V	V8	1966
N	383-2V	V8	1960
H	390-2V	V8	1964 to 1967
Y	390-2V	V8	1963 to 1967, 1969 and 1970
X	390-2V	V8	1968 and 1969 Premium fule
Z	390-4V	V8	1961 to 1966 and 1968

Fifth letter or number designates the engine type.

P   390-4V   V8   1962 to 1965 Police Special
S   390-4V   V8   1967 to 1969 GT model
M   396-4V   V8   1964 High Performance
B   406-4V   V8   1962 and 1963
G   406-6V   V8   1963
M   410-4V   V8   1966 and 1967
W   427-4V   V8   1966 to 1969
Q   427-4V   V8   1964
R   427-8V   V8   1964 to 1967
P   428-4V   V8   1966 to 1970 Police Special
Q   428-4V   V8   1966 to 1968
8   428-4V   V8   1967 Export model
Q   428-4V   V8   1969 and 1970 Cobra Jet
R   428-4V   V8   1969 Cobra Jet Ram Air
C   429-4V   V8   1970 Cobra Jet
K   429-2V   V8   1969 and 1970
N   429-2V   V8   1970 Thunderbird model
N   429-4V   V8   1969
Z   429-4V   V8   1970 High Output
M   430-4V   V8   1960

The last six numbers are the sequential production numbers.

OLDSMOBILE

1955 to 1964. V.I.N. plate is spot welded to the left front door hinge
1965 to 1967. V.I.N. plate is riveted to the left front door hinge post. (Illus. 32)
1968 to 1971. V.I.N. plate is located on the left side of the dashboard visible through the windshield. (Illus. 33 at B)

Assembly plants, their symbol designator and locations.

A   Atlanta, Ga.   1960 to 1964
B   Baltimore, Md.   1964 and 1965
C   Los Angeles, Calif.   1960 to 1963
C   Southgate, Calif.   1964 to 1970
D   Atlanta, Ga.   1965, 1966 and 1968
D   Doraville, Ga.   1969 and 1970
D   Kansas City, Mo.   1964
F   Fremont, Calif.   1964
G   Farmingham, Mass.   1966 to 1968 and 1970
K   Kansas City, Kan.   1960 to 1964
K   Kansas City, Mo.   1965
L   Linden, N.J.   1960 to 1970
M   Lansing, Mich.   1960 to 1970
R   Arlington, Tex.   1965
T   Arlington, Tex.   1960 to 1964
W   Wilmington, Del.   1960 to 1963
X   Kansas City, Kan.   1965 to 1968
X   Fairfax, Kan.   1969 and 1970
Z   Fremont, Calif   1965 to 1970

1960 to 1963.

Sample V.I.N. plate with number:

```
┌─────────────────────────────┐
│        OLDSMOBILE           │
│        635T123456           │
└─────────────────────────────┘
```

First two numbers designate the year model.
60 1960   62 1962
61 1961   63 1963

Third number designates the series.
1960
7   88   8   Super 88   9   98

1961 to 1963
0   F85 Standard
1   F85 Deluxe   6   Super 88 Starfire
2   88   8   98
5   Super 88   9   98 Sport coupe (1963)

Forth letter designates the assembly plant.

The last four or five numbers are the sequential production numbers.

1964.

Sample V.I.N. plate with number:

```
┌─────────────────────────────┐
│        OLDSMOBILE           │
│        874C123456           │
└─────────────────────────────┘
```

First number designates the engine type.
6   6 Cyl
8   V8

Second number designates the series model.
0   F85 std 3000 series
1   F85 dlx 3100 series
2   F85 Cutlass 3200 series
3   88 3300 series
4   Dynamic 88 3400 series
5   Super 88 3500 series
6   Starfire 3600 series
7   Jetstar I 3457 series
8   98 3800 series
9   98 Custom 3900 series

Third number designates the year model.
4   1964

Forth letter designates the assembly plant.

The last six numbers are the sequential production numbers.

1965 to 1971.

Sample V.I.N. plate with number:

```
┌─────────────────────────────────┐
│                                 │
│          336359C123456          │
│                                 │
└─────────────────────────────────┘
```

First number designates the Oldsmobile automobile.

3   Oldsmobile division of G.M.C.

The next four numbers designate the series and body style.

Body Style	1965 6 cyl	1965 V8	1966 6	1966 8	1967 6	1967 8	1968 6	1968 8	1969 6	1969 8	1970 6	1970 8
F85 Std												
2 dr cpe	3327	3427	3307	3407	3307	3407	3177	3277	3177	3277	3177	3277
4 dr sdn	3369	3469	3369	3469	3369	3469	3169	3269	—	—	—	—
4 dr sw 2 seat	3335	3435	3335	3435	3335	3435	—	—	—	—	—	—
Vista Cruiser SW 2 seat	—	3455	—	3455	—	—	—	—	—	—	—	—
Vista Cruiser SW 3 seat	—	3465	—	3465	—	3465	—	—	—	—	—	—
F85 Dlx												
2 dr ht	3527	—	3517	3617	—	—	—	—	—	—	—	—
4 dr ht	—	—	3539	3639	—	—	—	—	—	—	—	—
4 dr sdn	3569	3669	3569	3669	—	—	—	—	—	—	—	—
4 dr sw 2 seat	3535	3635	3535	3635	—	—	—	—	—	—	—	—
F85 Cutlass												
2 dr cpe	—	3827	—	3807	—	—	3577	3677	3577	3677	3577	3677
2 dr ht	—	3837	—	3817	3517	3617	3587	3687	3587	3687	3587	3687
4 dr sdn	—	—	—	3869	3569	3669	3569	3669	3569	3669	3569	3669
4 dr ht	—	—	—	3839	3539	3639	3539	3639	3539	3639	3539	3639
Convert	—	3867	—	3867	3567	3667	3567	3667	3567	3667	—	—
4 dr sw 2 seat	—	—	—	—	3535	3635	3535	3635	3535	3635	3535	3635
Vista Cruiser SW 2 seat	—	3855	—	3855	—	—	—	—	—	—	—	—
Vista Cruiser SW 3 seat	—	3865	—	3865	—	—	—	—	—	—	—	—

Body Style	1965	1966	1967	1968	1969	1970
Jetstar I						
2 dr cpe	5457	—	—	—	—	—
Jetstar 88						
2 dr ht	5237	5237	—	—	—	—
4 dr ht	5239	5239	—	—	—	—
4 dr sdn	5269	5269	—	—	—	—
Convert	5267	—	—	—	—	—

	1965 6 cyl	1965 V8	1966 6	1966 8	1967 6	1967 8	1968 6	1968 8	1969 6	1969 8	1970 6	1970 8
Dynamic 88												
2 dr ht		5637		5637		—		—		—		—
4 dr ht		5639		5639		—		—		—		—
4 dr sdn		5669		5669		—		—		—		—
Convert		5667		5667		—		—		—		—
Convert		5667		5667		—		—		—		—
Delta 88												
2 dr ht		5837		5837		—		—		5437		5437
4 dr ht		5839		5839		—		—		5439		5439
4 dr sdn		5869		5869		—		—		5469		5469
Convert		—		5867		—		—		5467		5467
Starfire												
2 dr ht		6657		5457		—		—		—		—
Convert		6667		—		—		—		—		—
98												
2 dr ht		8437		8437		8457		8457		8457		8457
4 dr ht		8439		8439		8439		8439		8439		8439
4 dr sdn		8469		8469		8469		8469		8469		8469
Convert		8467		8467		8467		8467		8467		8467
Lux sdn 4 dr		8669		8669		8669		8669		8669		8669
Lux sdn 4 dr ht		—		—		—		—		—		8639
Toronado												
2 dr ht		—		9487		9487		9487		9487		9487
2 dr ht dlx		—		9687		9687		9687		9687		—
F85 Cutlass Supreme												
2 dr cpe		—		—		3807		—		—		—
2 dr ht		—		—		3817		4287		4287		4257
4 dr ht		—		—		3939		4239		4239		4239
4 dr sdn		—		—		3869		4269		4269		—
Convert		—		—		3867		—		—		4267
F85 442												
2 dr cpe		—		—		—		4477		4477		4477
2 dr ht		—		—		—		4487		4487		4487
Convert		—		—		—		4467		4467		4467
F85 Custom sw Vista Cruiser												
2 seat		—		—		3855		4855		4855		4855
Vista Cruiser 3 seat		—		—		3865		4865		4865		4865
Delmont 88 330 eng												
2 dr ht		—		—		5287		5487		—		—
4 dr ht		—		—		5239		5439		—		—
4 dr sdn		—		—		5269		5469		—		—
Convert		—		—		—		5467		—		—

	1965 6 cyl	1965 V8	1966 6	1966 8	1967 6	1967 8	1968 6	1968 8	1969 6	1969 8	1970 6	1970 8
Delmont 88 **455 eng**												
2 dr ht		—		—		5687		5687		—		—
4 dr ht		—		—		5639		5639		—		—
4 dr sdn		—		—		5669		5669		—		—
Convert		—		—		5667		5667		—		—
Delta 88 **455 eng**												
2 dr ht		—		5837		5887		6487		—		—
4 dr ht		—		5839		5839		6439		—		—
Convert		—		5867		5867		—		—		—
Delta 88 **Custom**												
2 dr ht		—		—		5487		6687		6437		6437
4 dr ht		—		—		5439		6639		6439		6439
4 dr sdn		—		—		—		—		6469		6469
Delta 88 **Royale**												
2 dr ht		—		—		—		—		6647		6647

The sixth number designates the year model.

5	1965	8	1968	1	1971
6	1966	9	1969		
7	1967	0	1970		

Seventh letter designates the assembly plant.

The last six numbers are the sequential production numbers.

PLYMOUTH

1955 to 1964. V.I.N. plate is spot welded to the left front door hinge post. (Illus. 32)

1959. Some models have the V.I.N. plate located on the top of the cowl, left side, under the hood. (Illus. 48 at B)

1965 to 1967. V.I.N. plate is riveted to the left front door hinge post. (Illus. 32)

1968 to 1971. V.I.N. plate is located on the dashboard, left side, visible through the windshield. (Illus. 33 at B)

Assembly plants, their symbol designators and locations.
1   Detroit, Mich (Plymouth plant)   1960 to 1964
2   Detroit, Mich (Dodge plant)   1965
3   Detroit, Mich (Jefferson plant)   1960 to 1964 (except Valiant)
5   Los Angeles, Calif   1960 to 1967
6   Newark, Del   1960 to 1967
7   St. Louis, Mo   1960 to 1967
9   Windsor, Ontario, Canada   1967
A   Lynch Road, Mich   1968 to 1970
B   Hamtramck, Mich   1968 to 1970

D   Belvidere, Ill   1968 to 1970
E   Los Angeles, Calif   1968 to 1970
F   Newark, Del   1968 to 1970
G   St. Louis, Mo   1968 to 1970
R   Windsor, Ontario, Canada   1968 to 1970

1960 to 1964

Sample V.I.N. plate with number:

3305123456

First number designates engine type.

1   6 Cylinder   170
2   6 Cylinder   225
3   V8   318
3   V8   361

Second number designates series model.

PLYMOUTH
0   Fleet Special 1961 to 1963
1   Savoy 1960 to 1964
2   Belvedere 1960 to 1964
3   Fury 1960 to 1964
5   Savoy Suburban 1960 to 1964
6   Belvedere Suburban 1960 to 1964
7   Fury Suburban 1960 to 1964
8   Taxi 1960 to 1964
9   Police models 1962 to 1964

VALIANT
1   V100 Sedan 1960 to 1964
3   V200 Sedan 1960 to 1964
4   V200 Signet 1962 to 1964
5   V100 Station Wagon 1960 to 1964
7   V200 Station Wagon 1960 to 1964
8   Taxi 1961 to 1964

Third number designates the year model.

0   1960
1   1961
2   1962
3   1963
4   1964

Fourth number designates the assembly plant.

The last six numbers are the sequential production numbers.

1965

Sample V.I.N. plate with number:

First letter or number designates the car make and engine.

P	Fury	6 Cyl
R	Belvedere	6 Cyl
V	Valiant	6 Cyl
1	Valiant	V8
3	Belvedere	V8
5	Fury	V8

Second number designates the body series.
1   Valiant V100, Belvedere 1, Fury 1
2   Fury 2
3   Valiant V200, Belvedere 2, Fury 3
4   Valiant Signet, Belveder Satellite, Sport Fury
5   Valiant V100 Station Wagon, Belveder 1 Station wagon, Fury 1 station wagon
6   Fury 2 Station Wagon
7   Valiant V200 Station Wagon, Belvedere 2 Station Wagon, Fury 3 Station Wagon
8   Barracuda, Belvedere and Fury Taxi
9   Belvedere and Fury Police Models

Third number designates year model.
5   1965

Fourth number designates the assembly plant.

The last six numbers are the sequential production numbers.

1966 to 1971.

Sample V.I.N. plate with number:

BH23BOA123456

First letter designates model make.
B   Barracuda
P   Fury
R   Belvedere and Satellite
V   Valiant

Second letter designates the series model.
E   1967 Belvedere
    1967 to 1970 Fury 1
H   1966 Valiant V100
    1966 to 1969 Signet
    1967 to 1970 Barracuda
    1966 and 1967 Belvedere 2
    1968 to 1970 Satellite
    1966 Fury 3
    1967 to 1970 Sport Fury
K   1966 Fury and Belvedere Police models

Second letter designates the series model.

L   1966 to 1970 Valiant 100
     1970 Duster
     1968 to 1970 Belvedere
     1966 to 1967 Belvedere 1
     1966 Fury 1
     1967 to 1970 Fury 2
M   1967 to 1970 Fury 3
     1966 Fury 1
     1968 to 1970 Roadrunner
P   1967 to 1968 VIP
     1966 Sport Fury
     1966 Barracuda
     1970 Grand Coupe
     1966 to 1967 Satellite
     1968 to 1970 Sport Satellite
S   1967 to 1970 GTX
     1970 Sport Fury S23
     1968 and 1969 Sport Fury
     1966 VIP
     1970 Cuda
     1970 Duster
T   1966 to 1969 Taxi-Belvedere and Fury
X   1968 Fury 3 2 dr

Third and fourth numbers designate the body style.

21 1967 to 1969 Valiant Signet 2 dr sdn
     1966 to 1969 Valiant 100 2 dr sdn
     1968 to 1970 Roadrunner 2 dr sdn
     1966 and 1967 Belvedere 1 2 dr sdn
     1968 to 1970 Belvedere 2 dr sdn
     1966 to 1970 Fury 1 and 2 2 dr sdn
23 1966 to 1970 Satellite 2 dr ht
     1966 to 1970 GTX Belvedere 2 dr ht
     1966 to 1970 Fury 3 2 dr ht
     1966 to 1970 Sport Fury 2 dr ht
     1966 to 1970 VIP 2 dr ht
     1968 to 1970 Satellite sport cpe 2 dr ht
     1969 Roadrunner 2 dr ht
     1966 to 1970 Belvedere 2 2 dr ht
     1970 Grand Coupe 2 dr ht
     1967 to 1970 Barracuda 2 dr ht
     1969 and 1970 Cuda 2 dr ht
     1966 Signet 2 dr ht
27 1966 Signet Convertible
     1970 Grand Coupe Convertible
     1967 to 1970 Barracuda Convertible
     1970 Cuda Convertible
     1966 to 1970 Belvedere 2 Convertible
     1969 Roadrunner Convertible
     1968 and 1969 Sport Satellite and Satellite Convertible

Third and fourth numbers designate the body style.

        1966 to 1970 Fury 3 Convertible
        1967 to 1969 Belvedere GTX Convertible
        1966 to 1969 Sport Fury Convertible
29   1970 Sport Fury and 2 dr Special Sport Coupe
        1970 Fury 3 Sport Coupe
        1966 to 1969 Barracuda Sport Coupe
        1969 Cuda 340 Sport Coupe
        1970 Duster and Duster 340
41   1967 to 1969 Signet 4 dr sdn
        1970 Sport Fury
        1966 to 1970 Valiant 4 dr sdn
        1969 and 1970 Sport Satellite 4 dr sdn
        1968 to 1970 Belvedere 4 dr sdn
        1966 and 1967; 1969 and 1970 Fury 3 4 dr sdn
        1966 to 1970 Fury 1 and 2
        1968 to 1970 Satellite 4 dr sdn
43   1970 Sport Fury 4 dr ht sdn
        1966 to 1969 VIP 4 dr ht sdn
        1966 to 1970 Fury 3 4 dr ht sdn
45   1966 Signet 200 Station Wagon 2 seat
        1966 Valiant 100 Station Wagon 2 seat
        1966 to 1970 Belvedere 1 and 2 Station Wagon 2 seat
        1968 to 1970 Sport Satellite Station Wagon 2 seat
        1968 to 1970 Satellite Station Wagon 2 seat
        1966 to 1970 Fury 2 and 3 Station Wagon 2 seat
        1966 to 1969 Fury 1 Station Wagon 2 seat
        1970 Sport Fury Station Wagon 2 seat
46   1970 Sprot Fury Station Wagon 3 seat
        1966 to 1970 Fury 2 and 3 Station Wagon 3 seat
        1966 to 1969 Fury 1 Station Wagon 3 seat
        1968 to 1970 Satellite Station Wagon 3 seat
        1966 and 1967 Belvedere 2 Station Wagon 3 seat

Fifth letter designates the engine type.

A	6 Cyl	170	1966 to 1969
B	6	198	1970
B	6	225	1966 to 1969
C	6	225	1970
C	6	Special	1966 to 1969
D	V8	273	1966 to 1969
E	V8	273	1967
F	V8	318	1966 to 1969
F	V8	361	1966
G	V8	383	1966 to 1969
G	V8	318	1970
H	V8	383 HB	1967-to 1969
J	V8	440	1966
J	V8	429	1967 to 1969
K	V8	440	1967 to 1969
K	V8	Special	1969

Fifth letter designates the engine type.

L	V8	440 HP	1967 to 1969
L	V8	383	1970
M	V8	Special	1967 to 1969
N	V8	383 HP	1970
P	V8	340	1968 to 1969
T	V8	440	1970
U	V8	440 HP	1970

Sixth number designates the year model.

| 6 | 1966 | 8 | 1968 | 0 | 1970 |
| 7 | 1967 | 9 | 1969 | | |

Seventh letter designates the assembly plant.

The last six numbers are the sequential production numbers.

PONTIAC

1955 to 1964. The V.I.N. plate is spot welded to the left front door hinge post. (Illus. 32)

1965 to 1967. The V.I.N. plate is riveted to the left front door hinge post. (Illus. 32)

1968 to 1971. The V.I.N. plate is located on the left side of the dashboard visible through the windshield. (Illus. 33 at B)

Assembly plants.

A	Arlington, Tex	1960 to 1964
A	Atlanta, Ga	1955 to 1959
B	Baltimore, Md	1963 to 1970
C	South Gate, Calif	1955 to 1959 / 1965 to 1970
D	Doraville, Ga	1960 to 1970
E	Linden, N.J.	1965 to 1970
F	Farmingham, Mass	1955 to 1959
F	Freemont, Calif	1963 and 1964
G	Farmingham, Mass	1967 to 1969
K	Kansas City, Kan	1955 to 1964
K	Kansas City, Mo	1965 to 1968
L	Atlanta, Ga	1966 to 1970
L	Linden, N.J.	1955 to 1964
L	Van Nuys, Calif	1966 to 1970
M	Kansas City, Mo	1963 and 1964
P	Pontiac, Mich	1955 to 1970
R	Arlington, Tex	1960 to 1970
S	South Gate, Calif	1960 to 1964
T	Arlington, Tex	1955 to 1959 / 1965 and 1966
U	Lordstown, Ohio	1966 and 1968
W	Wilmington, Del	1955 to 1962
X	Kansas City, Kan	1965 to 1970
Z	Freemont, Calif	1965 to 1970
1	Oshawa, Ontario, Canada	1966 to 1970
2	Ste. Therese, Canada	1966 to 1970

1955 to 1958.

Sample V.I.N. plate with number:

```
┌─────────────────────────────┐
│         PONTIAC             │
│        A558H1234            │
└─────────────────────────────┘
```

First letter designates the assembly plant.

Second number designates the series model.

5	25 series	8	28 series
7	27 series		

Third and fourth numbers designate the year model.

55	1955	57	1957
56	1956	58	1958

Fifth letter designates the transmission type.

H	Hydramatic	S	Standard

The last four or five numbers are the sequential production numbers.

1959 to 1963.

Sample V.I.N. plate with number:

```
┌─────────────────────────────┐
│         PONTIAC             │
│        459K12345            │
└─────────────────────────────┘
```

First number designates the series model.

1959 and 1960.

1	21 series	4	24 series	8	28 series
3	23 series	7	27 series		

1961 to 1963

1	21	Tempest 1961 to 1963
2	22	Tempest La Mans 1963
3	23	Catalina 1961 to 1963
5	25	Ventura 1961
6	26	Star Chief 1961 to 1963
7	27	Bonneville Custom 1961 to 1963
8	28	Bonneville 1961 to 1963
9	29	Grand Prix Coupe 1962 and 1963

Second and third numbers designate the year model.

59	1959	61	1961	63	1963
60	1960	62	1962		

Fourth letter designates the assembly plant. Refer to listing of assembly plants.

The last four or five numbers are the sequential production numbers.

1964.

Sample V.I.N. plate with number:

> PONTIAC
> 844U1234

First number designates the series model.

0	Tempest	3	Catalina	9	Grand Prix
1	Tempest Custom	4	Star Chief		
2	La Mans	8	Bonneville		

Third number designates the year model.
4   1964

Fourth letter designates the assembly plant.

The last four or five numbers are the sequential production numbers.

1965 to 1971.

Sample V.I.N. plate with number:

> 242370L123456

First number designates the Pontiac automobile.
2   Pontiac division of G.M.C.

The next four numbers designate the body style.

Body Style	1965	1966	1967	1968	1969	1970
Tempest						
4 dr sdn	3369	3369	3369	3369	3369	3369
Sport Cpe	3327	3307	3307	3327	3327	3327
Safari SW 2 seat	3335	3335	3335	—	—	—
Tempest Custom						
4 dr sdn	3569	3569	3569	3569	3569	3569
Sport cpe	3527	3507	3507	3527	3527	3527
2 dr ht	3537	3517	3517	3537	3537	3537
4 dr ht	—	3539	3539	3539	3539	3539
Convert	3567	3567	3567	3567	3567	—
SW 2 seat	3535	3535	3535	3535	3535	3535
SW 2 seat Dual action tail gate	—	—	—	—	3536	—
Safari SW 2 seat dual action tail gate	—	—	—	—	3936	—
Safari SW 2 seat	—	—	3935	3935	—	—

Body Style	1965	1966	1967	1968	1969	1970
La Mans						
4 dr sdn	3769	—	—	—	—	—
Sport cpe	3727	3707	3707	3727	3727	3727
2 dr ht	3737	3717	3717	3737	3737	3737
4 dr ht	—	3739	3739	3739	3739	3739
Convert	3767	3767	3767	3767	3767	3767
SW 2 seat Dual action tail gate	—	—	—	—	—	3736
GTO 442						
Sport cpe	—	4207	4207	—	—	—
2 dr ht	—	4217	4217	4237	4237	4237
Convert	—	4267	4267	4267	4267	4267
Catalina						
2 dr sdn	5211	5211	5211	5211	—	—
4 dr sdn	5269	5269	5269	5269	5269	5269
4 dr ht	5239	5239	5239	5239	5239	5239
2 dr ht	5237	5237	5287	5287	5237	5237
Convert	5267	5267	5267	5267	5267	5267
Safari SW 2 seat	5235	5235	5235	5235	—	—
Safari SW 3 seat	5245	5245	5245	5245	—	—
SW 2 seat Dual action tail gate	—	—	—	—	5236	5236
SW 3 seat Dual action tail gate	—	—	—	—	5246	5246
2 + 2						
2 dr ht	—	5437	—	—	—	—
Convert	—	5467	—	—	—	—
Star Chief Executive						
4 dr sdn	5669	5669	5669	5669	5669	5669
4 dr ht	5639	5639	5639	5639	5639	5639
2 dr ht	—	5637	5687	5687	5637	5637
SW 2 seat	—	—	5635	5635	—	—
SW 2 seat Dual-action tail gate	—	—	—	—	5636	5636
SW 3 seat	—	—	5645	5645	—	—
SW 3 seat Dual action tail gate	—	—	—	—	5646	5646
Bonneville						
4 dr sdn	—	—	—	6269	6269	6269
4 dr ht	6239	6239	6239	6239	6239	6239
2 dr ht	6237	6237	6237	6237	6237	6237
Convert	6267	6267	6267	6267	6267	6267
Safari SW 3 seat	6245	6245	6245	6245	—	—
Safari SW 3 seat dual action tail gate	—	—	—	—	6246	6246

Body Style	1965	1966	1967	1968	1969	1970
Grand Prix						
HT cpe	6657	6657	6657	6657	7657	7657
Convert	—	—	6667	—	—	—
Firebird						
2 dr ht	—	—	2337	2337	2337	—
Convert	—	—	2367	2367	2367	—

Sixth number designates the year model.

5	1965	8	1968	1	1971
6	1966	9	1969		
7	1967	0	1970		

Seventh letter designates the assembly plant.

The next six numbers are the sequential production numbers.

IMPORTED VEHICLES

ALFA ROMEO (Italian)
1962 to 1969. V.I.N. is located on the firewall, right side or center, under the hood.
1970 and 1971. V.I.N. is located on the left wideshield post visible through the windshield. (Illus. 32 at C)

AUSTIN HEALEY AND SPRITE (English)
1960 to 1964. V.I.N. is located on the firewall under the hod.
1965 to 1969. V.I.N. is located on the left frame rail under the hood.
1970 and 1971. V.I.N. is located on the left windshield post visible through the windshield. (Illus. 32 at C)

B M W (German)
1968 and 1969. V.I.N. is located on the right front fender inner panel under the hood, left side of the firewall under the hood, along side of the right front suspension member under the hood, on the frame below the radiator under the hood, or on the rear wall of the luggage compartment.
1970 and 1971. V.I.N. is located on top of the steering column housing between the steering wheel and the dashboard visible through the windshield.

CITROEN (French)
1962 to 1969. V.I.N. is located on the firewall, right side, under the hood.
1970 and 1971. V.I.N. is located by opening the left front door and looking on the body panel near the top door hinge.
1970 and 1971 "All Purpose Vehicle" (Jeep type). V.I.N. is on the dashboard next to the speedometer.

DATSUN (Japan)
1962 to 1969. V.I.N. is located on the firewall or left front fender panel under the hood.
1969 to 1971. V.I.N. is located on the left side of the dashboard visible through the windshield. (Illus. 33 at B)

FERRARI (Italian)
The V.I.N. is located on the left front inner fender panel under the hood.

FIAT (Italian)
1960 to 1969. V.I.N. is located on the firewall stamped on the left side under the hood. A V.I.N. plate is also screwed to the firewall at this location.

1970 and 1971. V.I.N. is located on the dashboard, left side, visible through the windshield. (Illus 33 at B)

ENGLISH FORD
1960 to 1969. V.I.N. is located on the right front inner fender panel near the wheel suspension under the hood.

JAGUAR (English)
1960 to 1962. V.I.N. is located on the frame above the rear engine mount, left or right side front air vent, or on the firewall under the hood.

1963 to 1967. V.I.N. is located on the left or right lower side of the firewall under the hood.

1968 and 1969. V.I.N. is located on the hood latch panel under the hood.

1970 and 1971. V.I.N. is located on the upper portion of the left windshield post visible through the windshield. (Illus. 33 at D)

LOTUS (English)
1969 to 1962. V.I.N. is located on the right side brake air scoop under the hood.

1963 to 1969. V.I.N. located on the left side body panel under the hood.

1969 to 1971. V.I.N. is located on the dashboard in the center visible through the windshield. (Illus. 33 at E)

MASERATI (Italian)
V.I.N. is located on the firewall, upper left side, under the hood.

MERCEDES-BENZ (German)
1960 to 1967. V.I.N. is located on the right front inner fender panel, right or left side of the firewall, or on the hood lock panel near the radiator under the hood.

1968 and 1969. V.I.N. is located on the left front door striker plate post.

Illus. 51B

1970. V.I.N. is located on the left side of the dashboard visible through the windshield (Illus. 33 at C), left front door striker plate post (Illus. 33 at B), or on the frame rail, right side, towards the front under the hood.

M G (English)
1960 to 1969. V.I.N. is located on the inner front fender panel, left or right side, or on the firewall under the hood.

1970 and 1971. V.I.N. is located on the dashboard at center visible through the windshield. (Illus. 33 at E)

OPEL (German)
1960 to 1967. V.I.N. is located on the right front inner fender panel or on the left side of the firewall under the hood.

1968 to 1971. V.I.N. is located on the left side of the dashboard visible through the windshield or on the right side of the cowl under the hood.

PEUGEOT (French)
1960 to 1969. V.I.N. is located on the firewall, right side, under the hood.

1970 and 1971. V.I.N. is located on the left side of the dashboard visible through the windshield. (Illus. 33 at B)

PORSCHE (German)
1960 to 1963. V.I.N. is located on the left front door hinge post. (Illus. 32)
1964 to 1968. V.I.N. is located in the front luggage compartment near the gas tank.
1969 to 1971. V.I.N. is located on the left windshield post (Illus. 33 at C) and on the right side of the firewall under the hood.
1970 Audi. V.I.N. is located on the left side of the dashboard visible through the windshield. (Illus. 33B).
1971 Audi. V.I.N. is located on the left windshield post. (Illus. 33 at C)

RENAULT (French)
1960 to 1969. V.I.N. is located in the rear engine compartment.
1970 and 1971. V.I.N. is located on the left side of the dashboard visible through the windshield. (Illus. 33B), or in the rear engine compartment.

ROVER (English)
1960 to 1970. V.I.N. is located on the left front door hinge post (Ill. 32) or on the 1969 and 1970 models on the left front door striker plate post (Illus. 51 at B) and on the left front fender air vent tunnel.
1960 to 1970 Land Rover 88 inch wheel base (Jeep type) and 108 inch wheel base Safari. Left front door striker plate post or on a plate under the dashboard above the transmission cover.

SAAB (Sweden)
1960 to 1969. V.I.N. is located on the firewall, left side, under the hood.
1970 and 1971. V.I.N. is located on the left windshield post (Illus. 33 at C), left front door hinge post (Illus. 32), or left side of the firewall under the hood.

SIMCA (French)
1960 to 1964. V.I.N. is located on the tool box which is on the firewall, radiator support bracket, or left front inner fender panel under the hood.
1965 to 1968. V.I.N. is located on left rear inner body panel in rear engine compartment, or on the right inner front fender panel in the luggage compartment.
1969 to 1971. V.I.N. is located on the left side of the dashboard visible through the windshield. (Illus. 33 at B)

SUNBEAM (English)
1960 to 1968. V.I.N. is located on the radiator support bracket, hood locking panel, or on the firewall under the hood.
1970 and 1971. V.I.N. is located on the left windshield post visible through the windshield. (Illus. 33 at C)

TOYOTA AND TOYOPET (Japan)
1960 to 1969. V.I.N. is located on the radiator support bracket, on the firewall, under the hood, or on the left front door hinge post (Illus. 32)
1970 and 1971. V.I.N. is located on the dashboard, left side, visible through the windshield. (Illus. 33 at B)

TRIUMPH (English)
1960 to 1964. V.I.N. is located on firewall, right side, under the hood.
1965 to 1970. V.I.N. is located on left or right front inner fender panel under the hood.
1969 to 1971. V.I.N. is located on the left windshield post visible through the windshield. (Illus. 33 at C)

Illus. 55
Location of vehicle identification number in Bus. Panel, Pickup and Stationwagon—Volkswagon, 1955-1964.

Illus. 54
Location of vehicle identification number in 1955-1969 Volkswagon.

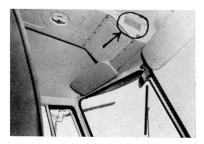

Illus. 56
Alternate location on some 1965-1971 models.

VOLKSWAGEN (German)

1955 to 1969. V.I.N. plate is located riveted to the body panel in the front luggage compartment behind the spare tire. (Illus. 54)

1955 to 1964 Bus, Panel, Pickup, and Station Wagon. V.I.N. is located stamped into the metal firewall to the right of the engine in the rear engine compartment. (Illus. 55)

1965 to 1971. Bus, Panel, Pickup, and Station Wagon. V.I.N. is located stamped into the metal floor pan to the right of the engine about half way between the door and the firewall in the rear engine compartment (Illus. 55). On some of these models, a plate bearing the V.I.N. may be found riveted to the right side of the air vent above the front seat (Illus. 56)

1970 and 1971. V.I.N. is located on the left side of the dashboard visible through the windshield. (Illus. 33 at B)

There is nothing about the V.I.N. of pre-1964 models to identify the body style or year model. The V.I.N. of post-1964 models describes the series as well as the year model.

The V.I.N.s listed below, for 1955 to 1964 models, indicate the year and the V.I.N. assigned to the vehicles manufactured that year.

1955: V.I.N. - 722,935 to 929,745
1956: V.I.N. - 929,746 to 1,246,618
1957: V.I.N. - 1,246,619 to 1,600,439
1958: V.I.N. - 1,600,440 to 2,007,615
1959: V.I.N. - 2,007,616 to 2,528,667
1960: V.I.N. - 2,528,668 to 3,192,506
1961: V.I.N. - 3,192,507 to 4,010,994
1962: V.I.N. - 4,010,995 to 4,846,835
1963: V.I.N. - 4,846,836 to 5,677,118
1964: V.I.N. - 5,677,119 to 6,502,399

The vehicle identification numbering system changed in 1965 to include the following information: The first two numbers designate the series and the third number the year model. The last six numbers are the sequential production numbers.

1965 to 1971.

Sample V.I.N.: 118-123456

Series Number	Description
11	2 dr "Bug"
14	Karmann Ghia
15	Convertible
21	Panel
22, 24 and 28	Station Wagons
23	Bus and Campmobile
26	Pickup
31	Fastback Coupe
36	Squareback sedan

Year designator	Year
5	1965
6	1966
7	1967
8	1968
9	1969
0	1970
1	1971

VOLVO (Sweden)

1960 to 1965. V.I.N. is located on the upper portion of the firewall on the right side under the hood.

1966 to 1968. V.I.N. is located on the left side of the firewall above the brake master cylinder under the hood.

1969 to 1971. V.I.N. plate is located on the left windshield visible through the windshield. (Illus. 33 at C)

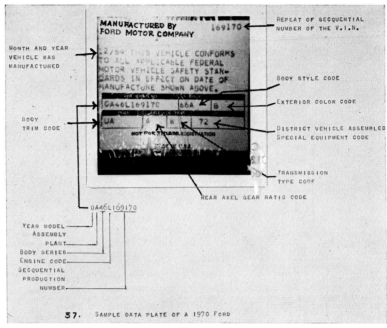

Illus. 57
Sample Data Plate of a 1970 Ford.

Vehicle Data Plates.

Many vehicles, both domestic and foreign, have vehicle data plates affixed to the body. On models up to 1968 these plates are metal and may be found on the firewall, a fender panel, the left front door, or the left front door hinge post. From 1969 these plates may be paper or a like material. The information on these plates describes the vehicle and its components thus allowing the investigator a supplemental means of identification. An illustration from a 1970 Ford is described in illustration 57.

Identification of Components

Engines

CHRYSLER PRODUCTS

1968 to 1971. Only engines designated as "high performance" are marked with identifying numbers. The engine number is located top left rear of block. The number consists of a letter designating the assembly plant, second number designating the year model (8 to 1), the third letter designates the vehicle type (V-Valiant, C-Chrysler), and the last six sequential production numbers from the V.I.N.

Sample Engine number: '9M123456

Sample V.I.N. CM27L9(3456

The engine size is stamp ı on top left face of block.

FORD PRODUCTS

1968 to 1971.

170, 200, 250 CI 6 Cyl. Number is located on the left side of block above the water temperature sender.

240 CI 6 Cyl. Number is located at rear of block below core plug.

289 and 302 CI V8. Number is located left rear of block below the head.

390, 427, 428, 462 CI V8. Number is located on the lower right side of the block below the head.

429 CI V8. Number is located on the right side at the front of the block below the alternator bracket.

The number should consist of the year designator, (8 to 1), assembly plant designator, and the sequential production number of the vehicle. Sample engine number: 1F123456

GENERAL MOTOR PRODUCTS

Buick 1968 to 1971

350 CI. Number is located on the left front face of the block above the fule pump.

400 and 430CI. Number is located on the left side near the front of the block.

Cadillac 1968 to 1971

Number is located on top of the block at the rear behind the intake manifold.

Chevrolet 1963 to 1967

All V8. Number is located on the right front of the block forward of the head. The number should consist of a year model designator (3 to 7), a letter designating the assembly plant, and the six sequential production numbers matching the V.I.N.

Sample engine number: 3L107639

Sample V.I.N. 31847L107639

1968 to 1971 (V8)

Number should be located at the same location as 1963 to 1967 models. The number is a little different in that the first number, 1, designates the Chevrolet automobile, the second number the year model, the letter and the six sequential production numbers as the earlier models.

Sample engine number: 19F107654

Sample V.I.N. 136379F107654

General Motors Sprint 1971 (V8)

Number is at the same location as the Chevrolet. Number should consist of 5 as the GM truck division designator, 1 for the year model designator, a letter for the plant designator and the six sequential production numbers.

Sample engine number: 51L105432
Sample V.I.N. 536801L105432
Pontiac 1968 to 1971
Number is located on the right front face of the block below the head.

Illus. 58
Location of identification marks on transmission.

Transmissions

CHRYSLER PRODUCTS

1968 to 1971. All 4 speed transmissions fastened to the "high perform-ance" engines should be numbered. The numbers should be the same as the engine and located right side of the case at lower center. (Illus. 58 at A) The automatic transmission is also numbered and the number should be located on top left front opposite the engine number.

FORD PRODUCTS

1968 to 1971. 3 and 4 speed transmissions. The number should be located on top of the transmission case on either left or right side at the front. (Illus. 58 at C) The automatic transmission is numbered either top rear or lower rear left side. The number should be the same as the engine.

GENERAL MOTORS PRODUCTS

1968 to 1971 all models.
Four speed transmissions should be numbered on left side. (Illus. 58 at B)

1963 to 1971 Chevrolet. Number should be on left side. (Illus. 58 at B)
1965 to 1967 Pontiac. Number should be on the top. (Illus. 58 at C or D)
1968 to 1971. All Turbo-Hydro transmissions should be numbered on the lower left center.
The Hydramatic transmission should be numbered on the right side. (Illus. 58)

Components Without Identification Numbers.

Many components stolen from vehicles will not be identified by an identification number. Some suggestions that the investigator may employ in an effort to identify them are outlined below.

Vehicles

The owner of a vehicle may recognize work he had done to the vehicle or other things he is familiar with. Special equipment, or the absence of it, dents, scratches, tears or worn spots in the upholstery, chipped or cracked glass, odd features about switches or gauges, or the speedometer mileage are all good points of identification.

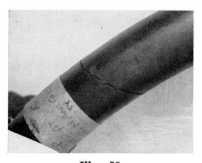

Illus. 59	Illus. 60
Comparison of tape covering wire loom linking it to stolen component.	Slashed motor hose matched to hose left on stripped vehicle.

Engine or Transmission.

Engines or transmissions not bearing identification numbers should be examined for cut wires, water hoses, or copper tubing. Illustration 59 shows the plastic tape covering of the wire loom found on an engine compared with the same tape on a wire loom found on the vehicle. Illustration 60 shows a cut water hose found on an engine also being compared with the remaining hose left on the vehicle. Both samples were sufficient to make positive identification of the engine as belonging to the vehicle.

Body parts

Body parts, fenders, hoods, doors, etc., can be connected to a vehicle by careful examination. Examination of the paint on the item with the paint on the vehicle may tie the item to the vehicle. If this method is used, the paint immediately adjacent to the suspected item must be used for comparison as the paint elsewhere on the vehicle may not be the same. Parts that are bolted in place are generally fastened by a bolt which is removable and a nut that is held in place by a clip, thus allowing for proper allignment by moving the part until it fits correctly in place. Suspected parts can be placed over the bolt holes and the allignment compared.

Wheels

Some individules who install special wheels on their vehicles paint the brake drum before installing the wheels. The side of the wheel which fits against the brake drum will have paint transfer from the drum. Since the person who painted the drum may have the remaining paint, this along with the sample found on the wheel and the drum can be used to make a positive connection.

Motorcycle Identification.

B.S.A. (England)

Prior to 1966 engine and frame number were not the same. Since 1966 engine and frame had the same number. The frame number is located on the left side of the diagonal frame bar below the goose neck. The engine number is located on the left side of the engine block below the cylinder.

It is important to note if the area where the engine number is stamped is a rough casting. This roughness is characteristic of the casting as it comes from the mold and should be the same over the entire engine case. A polished or smooth area under the number would suggest an alteration.

Sample V.I.N. A652L1234

Beginning with the 1969 models the numbering system on this motorcycle was changed. The V.I.N. now reflects the following information.

The first letter designates the month the motorcycle was manufactured.

A	January	E	May	K	September
B	February	G	June	N	October
C	March	H	July	P	November
D	April	J	August	X	December

The second letter designates the year of manufacture.

C	1969	H	1973	P	1977
D	1970	J	1974	X	1978
E	1971	K	1975	A	1979
G	1972	N	1976	B	1980

Note the absence of the letters F, I, L, M, and O to avoid confusion.

The next five numbers are the sequential production numbers.

The last combination of from three to five numbers and letters designate the model.

Firebird	A65F	Shooting Star	A44SS
Lightning	A65L	Starfire	B25S
Rocket	A75R	Thunderbolt	A65T
Royal Star	A50R	Victor Special	B44VS

Sample V.I.N.   AE12345A50R

Illus. 61
Location on pre 1970 model Harley Davidson motorcycles.

HARLEY DAVIDSON (U.S.A.)

Illustration 61 shows the location of the V.I.N. on pre 1970 models.

Sample V.I.N. 59FL1234

The first two numbers designate the year model (39-1939, 44-1944, 67-1967 etc.)

The next two to four letters (FL, XLCH) designates the series.

The last four or five numbers are the sequential production numbers.

1936 to 1948
U and UL 74 cubic inch engine
UH and ULH 80 cubic inch engine

1941 to 1951
45 cubic inch flat head engine for 2 wheel motorcycle. (Illus. 62)
W   WL   WLD   WLDR

1941 to 1971
45 cubic inch flat head engine for 3 wheel motorcycle.
G   GA   GD   GT

1964 to 1971 model with electric starter GE

1936 to 1947 Knuckle head (Illus. 63)
E and EL 61 cubic inch engine over head valve

1941 to 1947 Knuckle Head engine
F and FL 74 cubic inch engine over head valve

1948 to 1965 Pan Head engine (Illus. 64)
EL 61 cubic inch engine (1948 to 1952)
F and FL 74 cubic inch engine (1948 to 1965)
FLH 74 cubic inch engine (1955 to 1965)
FLE 74 cubic inch engine, police model, (1953 to 1969)

1966 to 1971 Shovel Head engine (Illus. 65)
FL and FLH 74 cubic inch engine
FX 74 cubic inch engine (1971)
NOTE: 1970 and 1971 FL, FLH, and FX models have no generator.

Sportster engine (Illus. 66)
K- KK- KRM 45 cubic inch flat head engine 1952 and 1953
KH and KHK 55 cubic inch flat head head engine 1954 to 1956
XL and XLH 55 cubic inch over head valve engine with battery ignition 1957 to 1971
XLH with electric starter 1967 to 1971
XLCH 55 cubic inch over head valve engine with magneto 1958 to 1969
XLCH 55 cubic inch over head valve engine with battery ignition 1970 and 1971

1970 and 1971. These models have a different numbering system. Beginning with the 1970 model both the engine and the frame are numbered with the same number.

Illustrations 67, 68 and 69 show some locations where these numbers will be found.
Sample V.I.N. 3A12345H1.

The first number-letter combination (3A) designates the model.
1A 74 CI engine (FLP, FLPH) frame number on right side of the frame on the vertical bar just below the goose neck.
2A 74 CI engine high performance (FLH, FLHF) frame number same as 1A.
3A 900 CC engine (XLH) Sportster with electric starter. Frame number same as 1A.

Illus. 62
Harley Davidson
Flat Head Engine.

Illus. 63
Harley Davidson Knuckle
Head Engine.

Illus. 64
Harley Davidson
Pan Head Engine.

Illus. 65
Harley Davidson
Shovel Head Engine.

Illus. 66
Harley Davidson
Sportster Engine.

Illus. 67.
Location of vehicle identification number on 1970 and 1971
Harley Davidson Motor Cycles.

4A 900 CC engine (XLCH) Sportster without electric starter. Frame number same as 1A.

5A 45 CI engine (GE) 3 wheeler. Frame number is same as 1A. Engine number located on right side of the engine between the distributor and exhaust pipe.

6A 350 CC Sprint. Frame number located on the left side of the goose neck. Engine number located lower left of block at the front.

7A MLS 125 Repedo. 125 CC engine. Frame number located on left side, lower center of motorcycle. Engine number located on left side at rear.

7B ERS 350 Scrambler. 350 CC engine. VIN same as 6A.

8A M65S Leggero. 65 CC engine. Frame number located on right side to rear of engine near foot peg. Engine number located on right side on block under the cylinder.

8B MSR Baja Scrambler. 100 CC engine. VIN same as 7A.

The next five numbers are the sequential production numbers.

The eighth letter, H, designates Harley Davidson Motorcycle Company.

The nine number, 0-1970, 1-1971, designates the year model.

Illus. 68
On the 1970-71 models the vehicle identification number may appear on both frame and motor.

Illus. 69
Alternate location of vehicle identification number
on 1970-71 models.

70   71

72   73

74   75

Illus. 70, 71, 72, 73, 74 and 75

Illustrate the various vehicle identification numbers used through the years.

Evidence of alteration to the V.I.N. are shown in illustrations 74 showing file marks across the boss, and illustration 75 at A showing a portion of the case having been ground off and (Illus. 75 at B) showing the irregular stamping of the number 2.

HONDA (Japan)

Honda motorcycles have a frame and engine number which are not the same.

Sample frame number: CB160   1234567

Sample engine number: CB160E   1234890

The last three digits of the two numbers may vary only slightly while the other numbers are the same. This suggests the frame and engine were numbered close to the same time. The letter E is only on the engine and designates engine.

The V.I.N. should be the frame number and is located on the left side of the goose neck. The engine number is stamped on a corrugated boss (Illus. 38). The V.I.N. consists of the model series and sequential production number.

Series	Description
Z50	50 CC Mini
S65	65 CC Mini
CL70	70 CC 17 inch wheels
CM70	70 CC step through frame
CT70	70 CC Mini
CA72	250 CC - 1 carb - Dream
CB72	250 CC - 2 carbs - Super Hawk
CL72	250 CC - 2 carbs - Scrambler
CA77	305 CC - 1 carb - Dream
CB77	305 CC Super Hawk
CT90	90 CC Trail 90
CB100	100 CC low exhaust pipe
CL100	100 CC Scrambler
SL100	100 CC high fenders
CB160	160 CC dual low exhaust pipes
CL160	160 CC Scrambler
CB175	175 CC Street model - dual exhaust pipes
CL175	175 CC Scrambler
SL175	175 CC high fenders
CB350	325 CC street model - dual exhaust pipes
CL350	325 CC Scrambler
SL350	325 CC high fenders
CB450	450 CC Dual over head cams - disc brakes
CL450	450 CC Scambler
CB750	750 CC 4 cyl - disc brakes

KAWASAKI (Japan)

Kawasaki motorcycles have both frame and engine numbers. Frame numbers are located on the right side of the goose neck and the engine number on the left top center of the block.

Model	Engine	Description
C2TR	120 CC	single cylinder trail m/c (red or red and silver)
F3	175 CC	single cylinder (silver in color)
F4	238 CC	single cylinder (purple and white or orange and white)
F21M	238 CC	single cylinder racing m/c
G3SS	90 CC	single cylinder low exhaust pipe
G3TR	90 CC	single cylinder high exhaust pipe
G4TR	100 CC	Scrambler

SUZUKI (Japan)

Suzuki motorcycles have both engine and frame numbers. Frame numbers are located on a plate riveted to the goose neck; on a plate riveted to the frame on the right side, top, forward of the rear shock absorber; on a plate riveted to the frame lower left center of the motorcycle; stamped on the frame shirt outer edge, left side, about axel height, about center of the motorcycle. Engine numbers are on top of the block either on the left or right side.

TRIUMPH (England)

Triumph motorcycles have both engine and frame numbers. They may or may not be the same. The frame number of the larger models is located on the left side of the goose neck or on the tube frame just below the goose neck. The engine number of the larger models is located the left side of the block below the cylinder.

The frame number of the smaller models is located on a plate which is riveted on the right side, below the seat, and forward of the shock absorber, or on the left side of the goose neck. The engine number is located on the front of the block at the front engine mount, on the right side below the cylinder, or towards the rear of the block on the right side.

Sample frame number: T105 12345

                              T 105
Sample engine numbers: T105 12345 or 12345

YAMAHA (Japan)

Yamaha motorcycles, except the 125CC and TD1 racing model, have numbers stamped on both the engine and the frame. The digits preceeding the sequential production number may vary but the sequential numbers should be the same on both.

Sample frame number: Y13-123456

Sample engine number: D5*123456

The frame number should be found on the left side of the goose neck on all models except the 100 which is on the right side.

The engine number is stamped on a corrugated boss.

Truck Identification

Chevrolet

1960 to 1964. The V.I.N. is spot welded on the left door hinge post about eye level height.

1965 to 1967. The V.I.N. plate is located on the top center door opening.

1968 to 1971. The V.I.N. is riveted on the left door striker plate post below the striker plate.

Dodge

1960 to 1971. The V.I.N. is riveted on the left door striker plate post below the striker plate.

Ford

1960 to 1971. The V.I.N. is stamped on the top of the right front frame rail forward of the cross member (Illus. 76 at A).

Bronco 1966 to 1971. The V.I.N. is stamped on the top of the right frame rail just below the firewall. (Illus. 76 at B).

General Motors Trucks

1960 to 1964. The V.I.N. plate is located on the left kick panel, forward of the door and under the dashboard inside the truck.

1965 to 1971. V.I.N. is riveted on the left door striker post below the striker plate.

Sprint 1971. This vehicle is identical to the Chevrolet El Camino except it has the G.M.C. body emblems on it. The V.I.N. is located on the left side of the dashboard visible through the windshield (Illus. 33 at B).

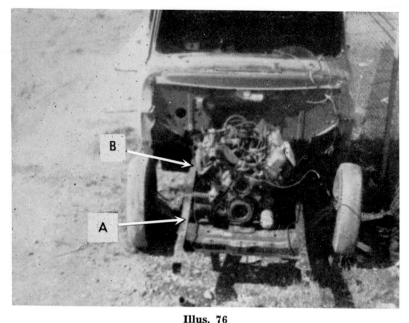

Illus. 76
Location of vehicle identification numbers on the Ford truck from 1960 to 1971.

The V.I.N. consists of the following information. First number, 5, designates the G.M. truck division.

The next four numbers designate the series.
3380   6 cyl Sprint
3480   V8 Sprint
3680   V8 Sprint Custom

The fifth number, 1, designates the year model, 1971.

The sixth letter designates the assembly plant.
B   Baltimore, Md.
K   Leeds, Kan.
L   Van Nuys, Calif.

The last six numbers are the sequential production numbers.

Sample V.I.N.   536801L123456.

International

1960 to 1971. V.I.N. is screwed on to the left door facing below the latch.

Refer to Chart 77 for the location of V.I.Ns. for other trucks.

Trailer Identification

Home made trailers in California are issued an identification number which should be stamped on the tongue.

Other small factory made trailers will bear an identification number stamped on the left or right side on the forward part of the frame behind the tongue.

An identification number plate may be found at this location rather than the stamping.

Refer to chart 78 for the location of V.I.N. of large trailers.

TRUCK VEHICLE IDENTIFICATION NUMBER LOCATIONS

MAKE	LOCATION
A.B.C.	C
American	5, 6
Birmingham	4, 6, 10
Brown	5
Butler	1
Copco	1, 9
Dorsey	4, 5
Fruehauf	1, 6
Galion	5
Gramm	8
Great Dane	A
Highway	1, 6, 7, 8
Hobbs	1, 3, 7, 8
Kentucky	7
Kingham	6, 8
Lufkin	3, 6
Nabors	A
Ohio	1
Peerless	7
Pike	3
Standard	7
Strick	9, 10
Timpte	7
Trailmobile	A, D, 1
Utility	5, 7

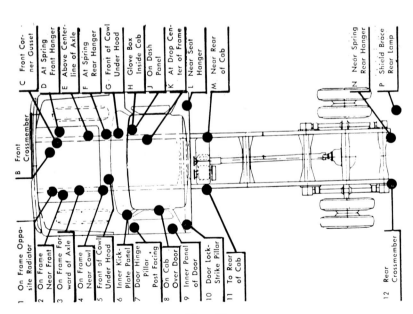

Illus. 77.
Courtesy National Auto Theft Bureau

TRAILER VEHICLE IDENTIFICATION NUMBER LOCATIONS

MAKE	LOCATION
Autocar	F, N, 9
Brockway	D, G, 5
Chevrolet	5, 6, 7, 8, 10
Crane	J
Diamond T	D, 4
Divco	C, K
Dodge	E, H, 7
Duplex	J, 8, 9
Federal	1, 2
Ford	D, P, 4
FWD	11
GMC	G, 5, 6, 7, 8, 10
Hendrickson	E
International	E, 2
Jeep	G, 5
Kenworth	D
KW-Dart	12
Mack	F
Marmon-Herrington	H
Peterbilt	J, M, 3
Reo	4
Walter	J
Ward-LaFrance	3
White	2, 3, 7

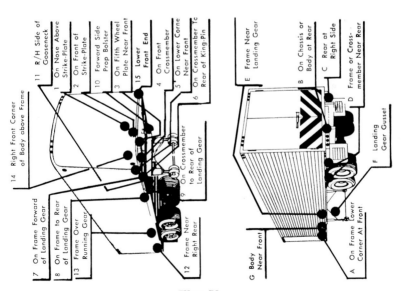

Illus. 78.
Courtesy National Auto Theft Bureau

. . . to the end.

INDEX

— N —

— O —

— P —

— Q —

— R —

Auto Theft Investigation

AMERICAN MOTORS

1970 to 1974.

Sample V.I.N. plate with number:

> A4A067E612345

The V.I.N. plate for the 1970 to 1974 models is located on top of dash, left side visible through the windshield.

First letter (A) designates American Motors.

Second Number (4) designates year model.

0 — 1970   1 — 1971   2 — 1972   3 — 1973   4 — 1974

Third letter (A) designates transmission type.

A	Automatic 3 speed column shift
C	1970 Javelin 3 speed floor mount (standard)
C	1970 automatic floor mount
C	1971-1974 automatic 3 speed floor mount
E	1970-1974 3 speed floor mount (standard)
F	1971-1974 3 speed floor mount (standard)
M	1970-1974 4 speed floor mount (standard)
S	1970-1974 3 speed column shift (standard)

Fourth number (0) designates series.

0	Hornet	1970-1974
1	Matador	1972-1974
1	Rebel	1970-1971
3	AMX	1970-1971
4	Gremlin	1970-1974
7	Javelin	1970-1974
8	Ambassador	1970-1974

Fifth number (6) designates body style.

3	1973 Hatchback
5	4 dr Sdn
6	2 dr Sdn
8	Station Wagon
9	2 dr Hardtop Coupe

Sixth number (7) designates body class.

0	Gremlin Basic	1970-1972
0	Hornet	1970-1971-1972
0	Rebel 550	1970-1971
1	Hornet SC360	1971
2	Ambassador	1970
2	Ambassador DPL	1971-1972
5	Ambassador DPL	1970
5	Ambassador	1973-1974
5	Ambassador SST	1971-1972
5	Gremlin 2 dr	1971-1972-1973-1974
5	Javelin	1970-1971-1972
7	Ambassador SST	1970
7	Ambassador Brougham	1971-1972-1973-1974
7	AMX	1970
7	Hatchback	1973-1974
7	Sportabout	1971-1972-1973-1974
7	Hornet Basic	1973-1974
7	Hornet SST	1970-1971-1972
7	Javelin Hardtop	1973-1974
7	Javelin SST	1970-1971-1972
7	Matador	1973-1974
7	Rebel SST	1970
7	Rebel Matador	1971
8	Javelin AMX	1971-1972-1973-1974

Seventh letter (E) designates engine type.

A	1970	199CI	6 Cyl	1 Brl Carb
A	1971-1974	258CI	6 Cyl	1 Brl Carb
B	1970	199CI	6 Cyl	1 Brl Carb
B	1972-1974	258CI	6 Cyl	1 Brl Carb
E	1970-1974	232CI	6 Cyl	1 Brl Carb
F	1970-1972-1973-1974	232CI	6 Cyl	1 Brl Carb
G	1970	232CI	6 Cyl	1 Brl Carb
H	1970-1974	304CI	V8	2 Brl Carb
M	1970-1974	304CI	V8	4 Brl Carb
N	1970-1974	360CI	V8	2 Brl Carb
P	1970-1974	360CI	V8	2 Brl Carb
S	1970	390CI	V8	2 Brl Carb
X	1970	390CI	V8	4 Brl Carb
Z	1971-1974	401CI	V8	4 Brl Carb
1	1970	304CI	V8	2 Brl Carb

Eighth number (6) designates assembly plant.
1 to 6 Kenosha, Wisconsin
7 to 9 Brampton, Ontario, Canada
Last five numbers are sequential production numbers.

AVANTI MOTORS CORP.

1969 to 1974.
Sample V.I.N. plant with number:

RQ-B2123

The V.I.N. plate for 1969-1970 vehicles is located riveted to left front door hinge post.

The V.I.N. plate for 1971 to 1974 vehicles is located top of dash left of center visible through the winshield.

First two letters (RQ) designates body style.
RQ   2 dr

Third Symbol is a hyphen (-).

Fourth letter (B) designates series.
A   Avanti
B   Avanti II

Last four numbers are sequential production numbers.

BUICK

1972 to 1974.
Sample V.I.N. plate with number:

```
4B17D4Z123456
```

The V.I.N. plate for 1970 throught 1974 models is located on top left side of dash visible through the windshield (illus. 33 at B).

First number (4) designates the Buick automobile.
4   Buick Division of GMC

Second letter (B) designates series.

B	1974	Apollo
D	1972	Skylark
D	1973-1974	Century 350
F	1972-1974	Century 350 Station Wagon
G	1972	GS
H	1972	Skylark
H	1973-1974	Century Luxus
J	1973-1974	Regal
K	1973-1974	Century Luxus Station Wagon
L	1972-1973	La Sabre
N	1972-1973	La Sabre Luxus
N	1974	La Sabre
P	1972-1973	Centurion
P	1974	La Sabre Luxus
R	1972-1974	Estate Wagon
T	1973-1974	Electra 225
U	1972	Electra 225
V	1972-1974	Electra 225 Custom
Y	1972-1974	Riviera

Third and fourth numbers (17) designates body type.

Apollo Body Type	1972	1973	1973
2 dr Hatchback	—	—	17
2 dr Cpe	—	—	27
4 dr Sdn	—	—	69
Century 350			
2 dr Cpe	—	37	37
4 dr Sdn	—	29	29
Gran Sport	—	—	37
Century Luxus			
2 dr Cpe	—	37	57
4 dr Sdn	—	29	29

Century Regal			
2 dr Cpe	—	—	57
4 dr Sdn	—	—	29

Sport Wagon Body Type	1972	1973	1974
Century 350			
4 dr 6 pass	—	35	35
4 dr 6 pass with dual action tail gate	36	—	—
Century Luxus			
4 dr 2 seat	—	35	35
Station Wagon			
4 dr 3 seat	—	—	45
Skylark			
2 dr Cpe	27	—	—
2 dr HT	37	—	—
4 dr Sdn	69	—	—
Regal			
2 dr Cpe	—	57	—
Skylark Custom			
2 dr Ht	37	—	—
4 dr	69	—	—
4 dr HT	39	—	—
Convert	67	—	—
GS			
2 dr HT	37	—	—
Convert	67	—	—
La Sabre			
2 dr HT	57	57	57
4 dr Sdn	69	69	69
4 dr HT	39	39	39
La Sabre Luxus			
2 dr HT	57	57	57
4 dr Sdn	69	69	69
4 dr HT	39	39	39
Convert	67	—	67
Centurion			
2 dr HT	47	57	—
4 dr	39	39	—
Convert	67	67	—
Estate Wagon			
4 dr 2 seat	35	35	35
4 dr 3 seat	45	45	45
Electra 225			
2 dr HT	37	37	37
4 dr HT	39	39	39
Electra 225 Custom			
2 dr HT	37	37	37
4 dr HT	39	39	39
Electra Limited			
2 dr HT	37	37	37
4 dr HT	39	39	39
Riviera			
2 dr HT	87	87	87

Fifth letter (D) designates engine.

D	1972-1974	250 CI	6 cyl	1 Brl Carb
G	1972-1974	350 CI	V8	2 Brl Carb Dual Exhaust
H	1973-1974	350 CI	V8	2 Brl Carb
K	1972-1974	350 CI	V8	4 Brl Carb Dual Exhaust
P	1972-1974	455 CI	V8	2 Brl Carb
R	1972-1974	455 CI	V8	2 Brl Carb Dual Exhaust
T	1972-1974	455 CI	V8	4 Brl Carb
U	1972-1974	455 CI	V8	4 Brl Carb Dual Exhaust
V	1972-1974	455 CI	V8	4 Brl Carb
W	1972-1974	455 CI	V8	4 Brl Carb

Sixth number (4) designates year Model.

2	1972
3	1973
4	1974

Seventh letter (Z) designates assembly plant.

C	1972-1974	Southgate, Calif
G	1972-1974	Framingham, Mass
H	1972-1974	Flint, Mich
L	1974	Van Nuys, Calif
N	1974	Norwood, Ohio
X	1972-1974	Fairfax, Kansas
Y	1972-1974	Wilmington, Del
Z	1972-1974	Fremont, Calif

The last six numbers are the sequential producton numbers.

CADILLAC

1972 to 1974.
Sample V.I.N. plate with number:

```
6D49S4E123456
```

The V.I.N. plate for the 1972 to 1974 models is located at left side of dash at the edge close to the windshield visible through the windshield.

First number (6) designates the Cadillac automobile.
6   Cadillac Division of GMC

Second letter (D) designates series.

B	1972-1974	Fleetwood Brougham
C	1972-1974	Calais
D	1972-1974	DeVille
F	1972-1974	Fleetwood 75
L	1972-1974	Fleetwood El Dorado
Z	1972-1974	Commercial Series

Third and Fourth Nnmbers (49) designates Body Type.

Body Type	1972	1973	1974
Calais			
2 dr	47	47	47
4 dr	49	49	49
DeVille			
2 dr	47	47	47
4 dr	49	49	49
Fleetwood Brougham	69	69	69

Fleetwood 75
4 dr   23   23   23
Limousine   33   33   33
Fleetwood El Dorado
2 dr   47   47   47
Convert   67   67   67
Commercial Series   90   90   90

Fifth letter (S) designates engine.
R   1972-1974   472 CI   4 Brl Carb.
S   1972-1974   500 CI   4 Brl Carb

Sixth number (4) designates year model.
2   1972
3   1973
4   1974

Seventh letter (E) designates assembly plant.
E   Linden, New Jersey
Q   Detroit, Michigan

The last six numbers are the sequential production numbers.

CHEVROLET

1972 to 1974.
Sample V.I.N. plate with number:

> IV77N4B123456

The V.I.N. plate for the 1972 to 1974 models is located on top of dash at left side visible through windshield.

First number (1) designates the Chevrolet automobile.
1   Chevrolet Division of GMC

Second letter (V) designates series.
B   1972   Chevelle Station Wagon
C   1972-1973   Chevelle and El Camino Deluxe
C   1974   Chevelle Malibu
D   1972   Chevelle and El Camino
D   1973-1974   Chevelle Malibu and El Camino Custom
E   1972-1974   Chevelle Laguna
G   1973-1974   Chevelle Malibu Estate Station Wagon
H   1972   Chevelle Concours Stn Wgn and El Camino Custom
H   1973   Chevelle Laguna Estate Station Wagon
H   1972-1974   Monte Carlo
K   1972   Biscayne
K   1973-1974   Bel Air
L   1972   Bel Air
L   1973-1974   Impala
M   1972   Impala
N   1972   Caprice
N   1973-1974   Caprice Classic and Estate Wagon
Q   1972-1974   Camaro
S   1973-1974   Camaro LT
V   1972-1974   Vega
X   1972-1974   Nova
Y   1973-1974   Nova Custom
Z   1972-1974   Corvette

6

Third and Fourth numbers (77) designate body type.

Body Type	1972	1973	1974
Vega			
2dr (4 cyl)	77	—	—
Hatchback 2 dr	—	77	77
2 dr Sdn	11	11	11
2 dr SW 2 seat	15	15	15
2 dr Panel Delivery	05	05	—
Nova			
Sport Coupe (6 or V8)	27	27	27
Hatchback 2 dr Cpe	—	17	17
4 dr Sdn	69	69	69
Custom Sprt Cpe	—	27	27
Cust Hatchbk 2 dr Cpe	—	17	17
Custom 4 dr Sdn	—	69	69
Camaro			
2 dr Cpe	87	87	87
2 dr Cpe LT	—	87	87
Chevelle			
Sport Coupe	37	—	—
4 dr Sdn	69	—	—
Deluxe 2 dr Cpe	—	37	—
Deluxe 4 dr Sdn	—	29	—
Deluxe 4 dr SW	—	35	—
Chevelle			
GMC Sprint PU	—	80	80
El Camino PU	—	80	80
El Camino 300 PU	80	—	—
El Camino Custom PU	80	80	80
Chevelle Laguna			
Sport Cpe	—	37	37
4 dr Sdn	—	29	—
4 dr SW	—	35	—
Estate 4 dr SW	—	35	—
Chevelle Malibu			
Spt Cpe	37	37	37
4 dr Sdn	69	—	—
Spt 4 dr Sdn	39	29	29
Convert	67	—	—
4 dr 2 seat SW	—	35	35
Estate 4 dr 2 seat SW	—	35	35
Nomad Datg	—	—	36
Chevelle Greenbrier			
4 dr SW 2 seat Datg	36	—	—
4 dr SW 3 seat Datg	46	—	—
Chevelle Concours			
4 dr SW 2 seat Datg	36	—	—
4 dr SW 3 seat Datg	46	—	—
Estate Wgn, 2 seat Datg	36	—	—
Est Wgn 3 Seat Datg	46	—	—
Monte Carlo			
Sport Cpe	57	57	57
Biscayne 4 dr Sdn	69	—	—
Brookwood			
4 dr SW 2 seat	—	—	35

Bel Air

4 dr Sdn	69	69	69
4 dr SW 2 seat	—	35	35
4 dr SW 3 seat	—	45	45

Townsman

4 dr SW 2 seat	35	—	—
4 dr SW 3 seat	45	—	—

Impala

Custom 2 dr Cpe	47	47	47
Sport 2 dr Cpe	57	57	57
Sport 4 dr Sdn	39	39	39
4 dr Sdn	69	69	69
Convert	67	—	—
4 dr SW 2 seat	—	35	35
4 dr SW 3 seat	—	45	45

Kingwood

4 dr SW 2 seat	35	—	—
4 dr SW 3 seat	45	—	—
Estate Wgn 2 seat	35	—	—
Estate Wgn 3 seat	45	—	—

Caprice

2 dr Cpe	47	—	—
4 dr Sdn	39	—	—

Caprice Classic

Spt. 2 dr Cpe	—	47	47
Spt. 4 dr Sdn	—	39	39
4 dr Sdn	—	69	69
Convert	—	67	67
Estate 4 dr SW 2 seat	—	35	35
Estate 4 dr SW 3 seat	—	45	45

Corvette

Stingray Cpe	37	37	37
Convert	67	67	67

Fifth letter (N) designates engines

A	1973-1974	140 CI	4 cyl	1 Brl Carb
B	1972	140 CI	4 cyl	1 or 2 Brl Carb
B	1973-1974	140 CI	4 cyl	2 Brl Carb
D	1972-1974	250 CI	6 cyl	1 Brb Carb
F	1972-1973	307 CI	V8	2 Brl Carb
H	1972-1974	350 CI	V8	2 Brl Carb
J	1972-1974	350 CI	V8	4Brl Carb
K	1972-1974	350 CI	V8	4 Brl Carb
L				
N	1974	110 CI	4 cyl	2 Brl Carb
R	1972-1974	400 CI	V8	2 Brl Carb
S	1972	400 CI	V8	4 Brl Carb
T	1973-1974	350 CI	V8	4 Brl Carb
U	1972	400 CI	V8	4 Brl Carb
U	1974	400 CI	V8	4 Brl Carb
V	1972	454 CI	V8	4 Brl Carb
W	1972	454 CI	V8	4 Brl Carb
X	1973	454 CI	V8	4 Brl Carb
Y	1973-1974	454 CI	V8	4 Brl Carb
Z	1973-1974	454 CI	V8	4 Brl Carb

Sixth number (4) designates year model.

2	1972
3	1973
4	1974

Seventh letter (B) designates assembly plant.

B	Baltimore Md
C	Southgate, Calif
D	Doraville
F	Flint, Mich
J	Janesville, Wisc
K	Leeds, Mo
L	Van Nuys, Calif
N	Norwood, Ohio
R	Arlington, Texas
S	St. Louis, Mo
T	Tarrytown, NY
U	Lordstown, Ohio
W	Willow Run, Mich
Y	Wilmington, Del
Z	Fremont, Calif
I	Oshawa, Ontario Canada
Z	Ste. Theresa, Quebeck, Canada

CHRYSLER

1971 to 1974.

Sample V.I.N. plates with numbers:

CE23T1F123456	CK23U4D123456
1971 to 1973	1974

The V.I.N. plate for the 1971-1974 models is located on top of dash at left side visible through windshield. Note: There is an asterisk at beginning and end of the V.I.N. The plate on the 1974 Chrysler Cars is small, as above, and does not include the Chrysler Emblem and Wording.

First letter (C) designates the Chrysler automobile.

C	Chrysler
Y	Imperial

Second letter (K) designates a special decor package for the 1974 models. The letters used are G, H, K, L, M, P, S, T. Contact local dealer. For exact description.

Second letter for the 1971 to 1973 models designates series.

E	1971	Newport
H	1971-1973	New Yorker
L	1971-1972	Newport Royal
L	1971	Newport Custom
L	1973	Newport
M	1971-1973	LeBaron
M	1972-1973	Newport Custom
P	1971-1973	Town & Country
S	1971	300
S	1972-1973	New Yorker Brougham

Third and fourth numbers (23) designate body type.

23	Newport 2 dr HT	1971, 1973, 1974
23	Newport Custom 2 dr HT	1971 to 1974
23	Newport Royal 2 dr HT	1971 and 1972
23	300 2 dr HT	1971
23	New Yorker 2 dr HT	1971 and 1972

9

23	New Yorker Brougham	1972 to 1974
23	Le Baron 2 dr HT	1971 to 1974
41	Newport 4 dr Sdn	1971, 1973, 1974
41	Newport Custom 4 dr Sdn	1971 to 1974
41	Newport Royal 4 dr Sdn	1971 and 1972
41	New Yorker 4 dr Sdn	1971 to 1974
41	New York Brougham 4 dr Sdn	1972 to 1974
43	Newport 4 dr HT Sdn	1971, 1973, 1974
43	Newport Custom 4dr HT Sdn	1971 to 1974
43	Newport Royal 4 dr HT Sdn	1971 and 1972
43	300 4 dr HT Sdn	1971
43	New Yorker 4 dr HT Sdn	1971 to 1974
43	New Yorker Brougham 4 dr HT Sdn	1972 to 1974
43	Le Baron 4 dr HT Sdn	1971 to 1974
45	Town & Country Stn Wgn 2 seat	1971, 1972, 1974
46	Town & Country Stn Wgn 3 seat	1971, 1972, 1974

Fifth letter (U) designates engine.

M	1972 to 1974	400 CI	V8	2 Brl Carb
T	1971 to 1974	440 CI	V8	2 Brl Carb
U	1973 and 1974	440 CI	V8	4 Brl Carb Hi-Perform

Sixth number (4) designates year model.

1	1971
2	1972
3	1973
4	1974

Seventh letter (D) designates assembly plant.

C	1971-1974	Detroit Mich
D	1971-1974	Belvidere, Del
F	1971	Newark, Del

Last Six numbers are the sequential production numbers.

DODGE

1971 to 1974.
Sample V.I.N. plates with numbers.

```
*DT41K4A123456*
```
CHRYSLER
CORPORATION

```
*DT41K4A123456*
```

1971 to 1973 All Models   1974 Monaco Models
1974 All Models except Monaco

The V.I.N. plate for the 1971 to 1974 models is located on top of dash at left side visible through windshield. Note: There is an asterisk at beginning and end of V.I.N. NOTE: Different V.I.N. Plate for 1974 Monoca models.

First letter (D) designates the Dodge Car.

D	1971-1974	Dodge standard
J	1973-1974	Dodge Specialty
L	1971	Dart
L	1973-1974	Dodge Compact
W	1971	Cornet and Challenger
W	1972-1974	Cornet and Charger (intermediate)

10

Second letter (T) designates a special decor package for the 1973 & 1974 models. The letters used are G, H, K, L, M, P, S, T. Contact local dealer for exact description.

Second letter for the 1971 and 1972 models designates series.

Second letter (T) designates a special decor package for the 1973 and 1974 models. The letters used are G, H, K, L, M, P, S, T. Contact local dealer for exact description.

E	1971	Polara
G	1972	New York Taxi
H	1971	Monaco, Dart Customs, Coronet 440, Charger
H	1971-1972	Demon 340, Dart Swinger, Charger
K	1971-1972	Police Coronet and Polara
L	1971	Cornet Deluxe, Dart, Polara, Swinger
L	1971-1972	Coronet, Demon, Dart
L	1972	Polara
M	1971	Charger, Demon 340, Polara Brougham, Super Bee, Swinger 360
M	1972	Coronet, Polara Custom
P	1971	Charger 500
P	1971	Coronet Brougham, Coronet 500, Charger 500
P	1971-1972	Charge SE, Coronet Crestwood
P	1972	Dart Custom, Challenger, Coronet Custom
S	1971	Charger RT, Polara, Coronet RT
S	1972	Polara
T	1971-1972	Coronet and Polara Tari

Third and Fourth Numbers (41) designate body type.

21	1972-1974	Charger 2 Dr Cpe
23	1971	Charger RT, Charger 500, Challenger RT, Coronet, Polara Brougham, Charger, Super Bee 2 dr HT Polara Brougham, Charger, Super Bee 2 dr HT
23	1971-1974	Dart Swinger, Monaco, Challenger 2 Dr HT
23	1972-1974	Dart Swinger Special, 2 dr HT
23	1971-1973	Polara, Polara Custom 2 dr HT
23	1972	Challenger Ralley 2 dr HT
23	1973	Monaco Brougham 2 Dr HT
27	1971	Challenger Convertible
29	1973-1974	Dart Sport, Dart Sport 360, 2 dr HT
29	1971-1972	Demon, Demon 360 2 dr HT
29	1971-1974	Charger SE Sport Cpe
41	1971-1974	Dart, Dart Custom, Coronet Custom, Polara, Monaco, 4 dr Sdn
41	1971	Coronet Brougham, 4 dr Sdn
41	1971-1972	Polara 4 dr Sdn
41	1974	Monaco Brougham 4 dr Sdn
43	1971	Polara Brougham 4 dr HT Sdn
43	1971-1974	Monaco 4 dr HT Sdn
43	1971-1973	Polara Custom 4 dr HT Sdn
43	1972	Polara 4 Dr HT Sdn
43	1974	Monaco Brougham 4 Dr HT Sdn
45	1971-1974	Coronet, Coronet Custom, Coronet Crestwood, Monaco, Stn Wgn 2 seat
45	1971-1973	Polara Custom and Special Stn Wgn 2 seat
45	1972-1973	Polara Stn Wgn 2 seat
45	1974	Monaco Brougham Stn Wgn 2 seat
46	1971-1974	Coronet Custom, Coronet Crestwood, Monaco Stn Wgn 3 seat
46	1971-1973	Polara Custom Stn Wgn 3 seat
46	1971-1972	Polara Special Stn Wgn 3 seat
46	1974	Monaco Brougham Stn Wgn 3 seat

Fifth letter (K) designates engine.

B	1971-1974	198 CI	6 cyl	
C	1971-1974	225 CI	6 cyl	
E	1971-1972	Special	6 cyl	
G	1971-1974	318 CI	V8	2 Brl Carb
H	1971-1972	340 CI	V8	4 Brl Carb
J	1974	360 CI	V8	4 Brl Carb
K	1971-1974	360 CI	V8	2 Brl Carb
L	1971	383 CI	V8	2 Brl Carb
L	1974	360 CI	V8	2 Brl Carb
M	1972-1974	400 CI	V8	2 Brl Carb
N	1971	383 CI	V8	4 Brl Carb Magnum
P	1972-1974	400 CI	V8	4 Brl Carb
R	1971	426 CI	V8	4 Brl Carb
T	1971-1974	440 CI	V8	4 Brl Carb
U	1971-1974	440 CI	V8	4 Brl Carb Magnum
V	1971-1972	440 CI	V8	3-2 Brl Carbs

Sixth number (4) designates year model.

1	1971
2	1972
3	1973
4	1974

Seventh letter (A) designates assembly plant.

A	1971-1974	Lynch Rd, Mich
B	1971-1974	Hamtramck, Mich
C	1971-1974	Detroit, Mich
D	1971-1974	Belvidere, Ill
E	1971-1972	Los Angeles, Calif
F	1971-1974	Newark, Del
G	1971-1974	St. Louis, Mo
H	1971-1973	New Stanton
R	1971-1973	Windsor, Ontario, Canada

The last six numbers are the sequential production numbers.

FORD

1971 to 1974.
Sample V.I.N. plate with number:

F4R05L123456F

The V.I.N. plate for the 1971 to 1974 models is located on top of the dash at the left side visible through the windshield. NOTE: The script letter "F" at the beginning and end of the V.I.N. Appear on all 1968 to 1974 Ford Vehicles except some 1969 to 1971 mustanges manufactured at the Dearborn, Michigan assembly plant (designated by letter F). This script is NOT part of the V.I.N.

First number (4) designates the year model.

1	1971
2	1972
3	1973
4	1974

Second letter (R) designates the assembly plant.

A	1971-1974	Atlanta, Georgia
B	1971-1974	Oakville, Ontario, Canada
D	1971	Dallas, Texas
E	1971-1974	Mahwah, NJ
F	1971-1974	Dearborn, Mich
G	1971-1974	Chicago, Ill
H	1971-1974	Lorain, Ohio
J	1971-1974	Los Angeles, Calif
K	1971-1974	Kansas City, Mo
N	1971-1974	Norfolk, Va
P	1971-1974	Twin Cities, Minn
R	1971-1974	San Jose, Calif
S	1971-1974	Pilot Plant, Mich
T	1971-1974	Metuchen, NJ
U	1971-1974	Louisville, Ky
W	1971-1974	Wayne, Mich
X	1971-1974	St. Thomas, Ontario, Canada
Y	1971-1974	Wixom, Mich
Z	1973-1974	St. Louis, Mo

Truck plants

C	1971	Ontario, Canada
L	1971-1972	Michigan Truck Assembly

Third and fourth number (05) designate body type.

01	1971-1973	Mustang 2 dr HT
01	1974	Mustang 3 dr Runabout
02	1971-1973	Mustang 2 dr Fastback
02	1974	Mustang 2 dr Notchback
03	1971-1974	Mustang Convertable
03	1974	Mustang 3 dr Runabout
04	1971-1973	Mustang Grande 2 dr HT
04	1974	Mustang Ghia
05	1971-1974	Mustang Mach 1 2 dr Fastback
10	1971-1974	Pinto 2 dr
11	1972-1974	Pinto 3 dr
12	1973-1974	Pinto 2 dr Stn Wgn
21	1974	Gran Torino Elite 2 dr HT
25	1971-1974	Torino 2 dr HT
27	1971-1974	Torino 4 dr HT Sdn
30	1971-1973	Gran Torino 2 dr HT
30	1974	Gran Torino, Torino GT, 2 dr HT
31	1971-1973	Gran Torino 4 dr HT Sdn
31	1974	Gran Torino, Torino GT 4 dr HT Sdn
32	1971	Gran Torino 4 dr HT Sdn
33	1971	Torino Brougham 2 dr HT
33	1974	Gran Torino Brougham 4 dr HT Sdn
34	1971	Gran Torino 2 dr HT Fastback
35	1971-1973	Gran Torino 2 dr HT Fastback
36	1971	Torino Brougham 4 dr HT Sdn
37	1971	Gran Torino Convertable
38	1971	Cobra 2 dr HT Fastback
38	1972-1973	Gran Torino 2 dr HT
38	1974	Gran Torino Sport 2 Dr HT
40	1971-1974	Torina Stn Wgn
42	1971	Torino 500 Stn Wgn
42	1972-1974	Gran Torino Stn Wgn
43	1971	Torino Squire
43	1972-1974	Gran Torino Squire
46	1971	Ranchero
47	1971-1974	Ranchero 500

48	1971-1974	Ranchero GT
49	1971-1974	Ranchero Squire
51	1971-1972	Custom 4 dr Sdn
52	1971-1973	Custom 500 2 dr HT (Canada only)
53	1971-1974	Custom 500 4 dr Sdn
54	1971-1974	Galaxie 500 4 dr Sdn
56	1971-1974	Galaxie 500 4 dr HT Sdn
32	1974	Gran Torino Brougham 2 dr HT
58	1971-1974	Galaxie 500 2 dr HT
61	1971-1972	LTD Convertable
62	1971-1974	LTD 2 dr HT
63	1971-1974	LTD 4 dr Sdn
64	1971-1974	LTD 4 dr HT Sdn
66	1971-1972-1974	LTD Brougham 4 dr Sdn
67	1971-1974	LTD Brougham 4 dr HT Sdn
68	1971-1974	LTD Brougham 2 dr HT
70	1971-1972	Custom Ranch Wagon 4 dr 2 seat
72	1971-1974	Custom 500 Ranch Wagon 4 dr 3 or 4 seat
74	1971-1974	Country Sedan 3 or 4 Seat (SW)
76	1971-1974	Country Squire 3 or 4 seat (SW)
83	1971	Thunderbird 1 dr HT
84	1971	Thunderbird 2 dr Landau
87	1971	Thunderbird 4 dr Landau
87	1972-1974	Thunderbird 2 dr HT
91	1971-1974	Maverick 2 dr
92	1971-1974	Maverick 4 dr
93	1971-1974	Maverick Grabber 2 dr

Fifth letter (L) designates engine.

A	1973-1974	460CI	V8	4 Brl Carb
B	1971-1972	240CI	6 Cyl	1 Brl Carb (Police)
C	1971	429CI	V8	4 Brl Carb
C	1973-1974	460CI	V8	4 Brl Carb (Police)
D	1971-1972	302CI	V8	2 Brl Carb (Police-Taxi)
E	1971-1972	240CI	6 Cyl	1 Brl Carb (Taxi)
F	1971-1974	302CI	V8	2 Brl Carb
G	1971	302CI	V8	4 Brl Carb High Performance
H	1971-1974	351CI	V8	2 Brl Carb
J	1971	429CI	V8	Corba Jet Ram Air
K	1971	429CI	V8	2 Brl Carb
L	1971-1974	250CI	6 Cyl	1 Brl Carb
M	1971	351CI	V8	4 Brl Carb
N	1971-1973	429CI	V8	4 Brl Carb
P	1971-1972	429CI	V8	4 Brl Carb (Police)
Q	1971-1974	351CI	V8	4 Brl Carb
R	1971	351CI	V8	4 Brl Carb (Boss)
R	1972-1973	351CI	V8	4 Brl Carb (High Perform)
S	1971-1974	400CI	V8	2 Brl Carb
T	1971-1974	200CI	6 Cyl	1 Brl Carb
U	1971-1972	170CI	6 Cyl	1 Brl Carb
V	1971-1972	240CI	6 Cyl	1 Brl Carb
W	1971-1973	1600CC	4 Cyl	1 Brl Carb
X	1971-1974	2000CC	4 Cyl	2 Brl Carb
Y	1971	390CI	V8	2 Brl Carb
Y	1974	2.3 Litre	4 Cyl	2 Brl Carb
Z	1974	2.8 Litre	6 Cyl	2 Brl Carb
2	1971-1972	200CI	6 Cyl	1 Brl Carb (Export)
3	1971-1974	250CI	6-Cyl	1 Brl Carb (Low Comp)
5	1971	240CI	6 Cyl	1 Brl Carb (Low Comp)
6	1971-1972	302CI	V8	2 Brl Carb (Low Comp)

The last six numbers are the sequential production numbers.

GMC SPRINT

The GMC Sprint pickup is similar to the Chevrolet El Camino.

1971 and 1972.

Sample V.I.N. (see page 210).

536801L123456

1973 and 1974

5D80N4L123456

First number (5) designates the GMC model.
5   GMC division of General Motors Corp.

Second letter (D) designates series.
D   1973-1974   Sprint

Third and forth numbers (80) designates body type.
80   1973-1974   GMC Sprint pickup

Fifth letter (N) designates engine.
(See Chevrolet)

Sixth number (4) designates the year model.
3   1973
4   1974

Seventh letter (L) designates assembly plant.
(See Chevrolet)

Last six numbers are the sequential production numbers.

JEEP

1972-1974

Sample V.I.N. plate with number:

JEEP
J4M835TA12345

The V.I.N. plate for Jeep vehicles is riveted to the upper left side of the firewall or on the left front door hinge post.

First letter (J) designates Jeep Company.

Second number (4) designates the year model.
2   1972
3   1973
4   1974

15

Third letter (M) designates the assembly plant, type of transmission and if left or right hand drive.

	Plant	Transmission	Drive Position
A	Toledo	automatic	LHD
B	CKD	automatic	LHD
F	Toledo	3 speed	LHD
G	Toledo	3 speed	RHD
J	CKD	3 speed	LHD
K	CKD	3 speed	RHD
M	Toledo	4 speed	LHD
N	Toledo	4 speed	RHD
O	CKD	4 speed	LHD
P	CKD	4 speed	RHD

Fourth and fifth numbers (83) designates body line.

14	Wagoneer	110 inch wheel base
24	Truck	120 inch wheel base
34	Truck	132 inch wheel base
63	CJ5	81 inch wheel base (CKD)
64	CJ6	101 inch wheel base (CKD)
71	MO	Government built vehicles
72	MDA	Government built vehicles
78	M606	Government built vehicles
83	CJ5	84 inch wheel base
84	CJ6	104 inch wheel base
87	Commando	104 inch wheel base

Sixth number (5) designates body style.

1	Thriftside truck
2	Townside truck
3	Platform stake truck
4	4 dr station wagon
5	Open body
6	Cab and chassis
8	Stripped chassis
F	Full metal cab
H	Half metal cab

Seventh letter (T) designates body type with weight.

	Type		Weight (GVW)
C	Custom Wagon		5400 lbs
O	Standard Wagon		5400 lbs
R	CJ6	(max)	4750 lbs
S	CJ5	(max)	4500 lbs
T	CJ5	(std)	3750 lbs
U	Commando	(max)	4700 lbs
V	Commando CJ6		3900 lbs
W	Truck		5000 lbs
X	Truck		6000 lbs
Y	Truck		7000 lbs
Z	Truck		8000 lbs

Eighth letter (A) designates engine.

A	258CI	6 Cyl	Regular
B	258CI	6 Cyl	Low Compression
E	232CI	6 Cyl	Regular Compression
F	232CI	6 Cyl	Low Compression
H	304CI	V8	Regular Compression
N	360CI	V8	Regular Compression
R	134CI	4 Cyl	Regular Compression
T	134CI	4 Cyl	Low Compression

The last five numbers are the sequential production numbers.

LINCOLN

1972 to 1974.

Sample V.I.N. plate with number:

```
F 4Y82A123456 F
```

The V.I.N. plate for the 1972 to 1974 models is located on top of dash at the left side visible through the winshield.
NOTE: The script letter *"F"* at the beginning and end of the V.I.N. appear on all 1968 to 1974 Lincoln vehicles. This script is *NOT* part of the V.I.N.

First number (4) designates the year model.

2   1972
3   1973
4   1974

Second letter (Y) designates assembly plant.

S   Pilot plant, Mich.
Y   Wixom, Mich.

Third and fourth numbers (82) designates body type.

81	1972-1974	Continental	2 dr HT
82	1972-1974	Continental	4 dr HT Sdn
89	1972-1974	Mark IV	2 dr HT

Fifth letter (A) designates engine.

A   1972-1974   460CI   V8   4 Brl Carb

Last six numbers are the sequential production numbers.

MERCURY

1971 to 1974.

Sample V.I.N. plate with number:

```
F 4F30T123456 F
```

The V.I.N. plate for the 1971 to 1974 models is located on top of dash at left side visible through the windshield.
NOTE: The script letter *"F"* at the beginning and end of the V.I.N. appear on all 1968 to 1974 Mercury vehicles. This script is *NOT* part of the V.I.N.

First number (4) designates the year model.

1   1971
2   1972
3   1973
4   1974

Second letter (F) designates the assembly plant.

B	1971-1974	Oakville, Ontario, Canada
F	1971-1974	Dearborn, Michigan
H	1971-1974	Lorain, Ohio
K	1971-1974	Kansas City, Missouri
S	1971-1974	Pilot Plant, Michigan
Z	1971-1974	St. Louis, Missouri

Third and fourth numbers (30) designates body type.

01	1971	Montego	2 dr HT
02	1971	Montego	4 dr Sdn
02	1972-1974	Montego	4 dr HT Sdn
03	1972-1974	Montego	2 dr HT
04	1972-1974	Montego MX	4 dr HT Sdn
05	1971	Montego MX	4 dr Sdn
05	1972-1973	Montego MX	2 dr Fastback
07	1971-1974	Montego MX	2 dr HT
08	1971-1974	Montego MX	Stn Wgn
10	1971	Montego MX Brougham	4 dr Sdn
10	1972-1974	Montego Brougham	4 dr Sdn
11	1971	Montego MX Brougham	2 dr HT
11	1972-1974	Montego Brougham	2 dr HT
12	1971	Montego MX Brougham	4 dr HT Sdn
15	1971	Montego Cyclone	2 dr HT
16	1971	Montego Cyclone GT	2 dr HT
17	1971	Montego Cyclone Spoiler	2 dr HT
18	1971-1974	Montego MX Villager	Stn Wgn
40	1971	Marquis	4 dr HT Sdn
40	1972-1974	Marquis	4 dr Sdn
41	1971-1974	Marquis	2 dr HT
42	1971-1974	Marquis	4 dr HT Sdn
44	1971	Monterey	4 dr Sdn
44	1972-1974	Monterey	4 dr HT Sdn
46	1971-1974	Monterey	2 dr HT
48	1971-1973	Monterey	4 dr HT Sdn
54	1971	Monterey Custom	4 dr Sdn
54	1972-1974	Monterey Custom	4 dr HT Sdn
56	1971-1974	Monterey Custom	2 dr HT
58	1971-1973	Monterey Custom	4 dr HT Sdn
62	1971	Marquis Brougham	4 dr HT Sdn
62	1972-1974	Marquis Brougham	4 dr Sdn
63	1971	Marquis	4 dr HT Sdn
63	1972-1974	Marquis	4 dr Sdn
64	1971-1974	Marquis Brougham	2 dr HT
66	1971-1974	Marquis Brougham	2 dr HT
67	1971-1974	Marquis Brougham	4 dr HT Sdn
68	1971-1974	Marquis	4 dr HT Sdn
72	1971-1974	Monterey	4 dr Stn Wgn
74	1971-1974	Monterey	4 dr Stn Wgn
76	1971-1974	Colony Park	4 dr Stn Wgn
91	1971-1973	Cougar	2 dr HT
92	1971-1973	Cougar	Convert
93	1971-1974	Cougar XR7	2 dr HT
94	1971-1973	Cougar XR7	Convert

Fifth letter (T) designates engine.

A	1973-1974	460CI	V8	4 Brl Carb
C	1971	429CI	V8	4 Brl Carb (Cobra Jet)
C	1973-1974	460CI	V8	4 Brl Carb (Police)
D	1971	302CI	V8	2 Brl Carb (Taxi)
F	1971-1974	302CI	V8	2 Brl Carb
H	1971-1974	351CI	V8	2 Brl Carb
J	1971	429CI	V8	4 Brl Carb (Cobra Jet Ram Air)
K	1971	429CI	V8	2 Brl Carb
L	1971-1974	250CI	6 Cyl	1 Brl Carb
M	1971	351CI	V8	4 Brl Carb
N	1971-1973	429CI	V8	4 Brl Carb
P	1972	429CI	V8	4 Brl Carb (Police)
Q	1971-1974	351CI	V8	4 Brl Carb
S	1971-1974	400CI	V8	2 Brl Carb

T	1971-1974	200CI	6 Cyl	1 Brl Carb
U	1971-1972	170CI	6 Cyl	1 Brl Carb
3	1971-1972	250CI	6 Cyl	1 Brl Carb (Export)
6	1971-1972	302CI	V8	2 Brl Carb (Export)

The last six numbers are the sequential production numbers.

OLDSMOBILE

1972 to 1974.

Sample V.I.N. with number:

```
3B17D45123456
```

The V.I.N. plate for the 1972 to 1974 models is located top of dash at left side visible through windshield.

First number (3) designates the Oldsmobile car.

3   Oldsmobile division of GMC

Second letter (B) designates series.

B	1973-1974	Omega
D	1972	F85
F	1972	Cutlass Standard
F	1973-1974	Cutlass
G	1972-1974	Cutlass
H	1974	Cutlass Supreme
J	1972-1974	Cutlass Supreme
J	1973-1974	Vista Cruiser
K	1972	Vista Cruiser
L	1972-1974	Delta 88
N	1972-1974	Delta 88 Royale
Q	1973-1974	Custom Cruiser
R	1972-1974	Custom Cruiser
T	1972	Special Chassis
T	1973-1974	98
U	1972	98
U	1973-1974	Toronado Chassis
V	1972-1974	98 Luxury
W	1973-1974	Special Chassis
X	1972	Toronado Chasis
X	1973-1974	98 Regency

Third and fourth numbers (17) designates body type.

17	1973-1974	Omega 2 dr Hatchback
27	1973-1974	Omega 2 dr Cpe
27	1974	Cutlass Supreme Colonnade 4 dr Sdn
29	1973	Cutlass Supreme Colonnade 4 dr Sdn
29	1973-1974	Cutlass Colonnade 4 dr Sdn
35	1973-1974	Delta 88 Custom Crusier Stn Wgn 2 seat
35	1972	Delta 88 455CI engine Stn Wgn 2 seat
35	1973-1974	Cutlass Supreme Stn Wgn 2 seat
36	1972	Cutlass 4 dr Stn Wgn 2-seat
37	1973-1974	Cutlass Colonnade 2 dr HT and Cutlass S Colonnade 2 dr HT
37	1972-1974	98 2 dr HT (all models)
39	1972	Cutlass Supreme 4 dr HT Sdn
39	1972-1974	98, Delta 88 and Royale 4 dr HT Sdn
45	1972	Delta 88 Stn Wgn 3 seat
45	1972-1974	Delta 88 Custom and Cutlass Supreme Stn Wgn 3 seat

19

51	1972-1974	Toronado Special Order Chassis
56	1972	F85 Vista Crusier 2 seat
57	1972-1974	Cutlass Supreme, Delta 88, Delta 88 Royale,Toronado and Toronado Brougham 2 dr HT
60	1972-1974	Toronado Special Order Chassis
66	1972	F85 Vista Cruiser 2 seat
67	1972-1974	Delta 88 Royale Convert
67	1972	Cutlass Supreme Convert
69	1972-1974	Delta 88 Royale, Delta 88 4 dr Sdn
69	1973-1974	Omega 4 dr Sdn
69	1972	F85 and Cutlass 4 dr Sdn
77	1972	Cutlass S 2 dr
87	1972	Cutlass S and F85 2 dr HT

Fifth letter (D) designates engine.

D	1973-1974	250CI	6 Cyl	1 Brl Carb
H	1972-1973	350CI	V8	2 Brl Carb
I	1974	455CI	V8	4 Brl Carb
J	1972	350CI	V8	2 Brl Carb
K	1973-1974	350CI	V8	4 Brl Carb
M	1972-1974	350CI	V8	4 Brl Carb (dual exhaust)
T	1972-1973	455CI	V8	4 Brl Carb
U	1972-1974	455CI	V8	4 Brl Carb (dual exhaust)
V	1972-1973	455CI	V8	4 Brl Carb (dual exhaust)
W	1972-1974	455CI	V8	4 Brl Carb
X	1972	455CI	V8	4 Brl Carb

Sixth number (4) designates year model.

2	1972
3	1973
4	1974

Seventh letter (L) designates assembly plant.

D	1974	Doravilla, Ga.
E	1972-1974	Linden, N.J.
G	1972-1974	Framingham, Mass.
L	1973-1974	Van Nuys, Calif.
M	1972-1974	Lansing, Mich.
R	1972-1974	Arlington, Tex.
W	1973-1974	Willow Run, Mich.
X	1972-1974	Fairfax, Kan.
Z	1972	Fremont, Calif.

Last six numbers are the sequential production numbers.

PLYMOUTH

1971 to 1974

Sample V.I.N. plates with numbers:

RH23B4A123456

* BH43K4A123456 *

1974 Fury models

1971 to 1973 all models
1974 all models except Fury
1974 Fury models

The V.I.N. plate for 1971 to 1974 models is located top of dash left side visible through the windshield.

NOTE: Different V.I.N. plate used for 1974 Fury models and asterisks at beginning and end of V.I.N.

First letter (B) designates Plymouth car.

B	1971-1972	Barracuda
B	1973-1974	Plymouth (Specialty)
P	1972-1974	Plymouth (Standard)
P	1971	Fury
R	1971-1974	Belvedere and Satellite (Intermediate)
V	1972	Valiant
V	1973	Compacts

Second letter (H) designates body series and vary with each car according to special equipment. Contact dealer for description for 1973 and 1974 models.

Second letter (H) for 1971 and 1972 models designates body series.

E	1971-1972	Fury I
H	1971-1972	Scamp, Barracuda, Satellite Custom, and Satellite Sebring
H	1972	Fury III and Custom Suburban
H	1971	Sport Fury
K	1971-1972	Police
L	1971	Fury II
L	1972	Fury I and Scamp Special
L	1971-1972	Satellite, Duster and Valiant
M	1971	Fury III
M	1972	Fury II
M	1971-1972	Road Runner
P	1971	Sport Fury GT, Gran Coupe & Satellite Brougham
P	1971-1972	Satellite Sebring, Satellite Regent
P	1972	Gran Coupe, Gran Sedan, and Sport Suburban
S	1971-1972	Duster 340 and Cuda
S	1971	AAR Cuda and GTX
T	1971-1972	Taxi

Third and fourth numbers (23) designates body type.

21	1971	Fury I 2 dr
21	1972-1974	Satellite 2 dr
21	1973-1974	Road Runner 2 dr
23	1971	Barracuda Sport Cupe, Barracuda Gran Coupe, Satellite Coupe, Sport Fury, Sport Fury GT 2 dr HT
23	1971-1974	Scamp, Barracuda, Cuda, Satellite Sebring, and Fury
23	1971-1972	Roadrunner, Fury II 2 dr HT
23	1972-1974	Fury Gran Coupe 2 dr HT
27	1971	Barracuda Convert
29	1971-1974	Duster 2 dr
29	1971-1972	Fury III 2 dr
29	1971	Sport Fury 2 dr
29	1972	Gran Coupe 2 dr
41	1971	Sport Fury, Satellite Brougham 4 dr Sdn
41	1971-1974	Valiant, Satellite, Fury I, II, III 4 dr Sdn
43	1971	Sport Fury
43	1971-1974	Fury III 4 dr HT Sdn
43	1972-1974	Fury Gran Sedan 4 dr HT Sdn
45	1971-1974	Satellite Stn Wgn 2 seat
45	1971	Fury II, III, Sport Fury Stn Wgn 2 seat
45	1973	Fury III Stn Wgn 2 seat
45	1972-1974	Custom and Sport Suburban Stn Wgn 2 seat
45	1973-1974	Fury II Stn Wgn 2 seat
46	1971	Sport Fury, Fury II, III Stn Wgn 3 seat
46	1973 Fury III Stn Wgn 3 seat	
46	1971-1974	Satellite Stn Wgn 3 seat
46	1972-1974	Custom and Sport Suburban Stn Wgn 3 seat

Fifth letter (B) designates engine.

B	1971-1974	198CI	6 Cyl	
C	1971-1974	225CI	6 Cyl	
G	1971-1974	318CI	V8	
H	1971-1974	340CI	V8	High Performance
J	1974	360CI	V8	4 Brl Carb
K	1972-1974	360CI	V8	
L	1974	360CI	V8	
L	1971	383CI	V8	
M	1972-1974	400CI	V8	
P	1972-1974	400CI	V8	4 Brl Carb
T	1972-1974	440CI	V8	
U	1971-1974	440CI	V8	4 Brl Carb (High Performance)
V	1971-1972	440CI	V8	3-2 Brl Carbs

Sixth number (4) designates year model.

1	1971
2	1972
3	1973
4	1974

Seventh letter (A) designates assembly plant.

A	1971-1974	Detroit, Mich.
B	1971-1974	Hamtramck, Mich.
C	1974	Detroit, Mich.
D	1971-1974	Belvidere, Ill.
E	1971	Los Angeles, Calif.
F	1971-1974	Newark, Del.
G	1971-1974	St. Louis, Mo.
R	1971-1974	Windsor, Ontario, Canada
5	1974	Japan
9	1974	Japan

The last six numbers are the sequential production numbers.

PONTIAC

1972 to 1974.
Sample V.I.N. plate with number:

```
┌─────────────────────────────┐
│                             │
│     2Y69A4A123456           │
│                             │
└─────────────────────────────┘
```

The V.I.N. plate for the 1972 to 1974 models is located top of dash at left side visible through the winshield.

First number (2) designates the Pontiac car.

2   Pontiac division of GMC

Second letter (Y) designates body series.

D	1972-1974	Le Mans
D	1972	Le Mans Sport
F	1973-1974	Le Mans Sport
G	1972-1974	Le Mans Luxury
H	1973-1974	Grand Am
K	1972-1974	Grand Prix
L	1972-1974	Catalina
M	1972	Catalina Brougham
N	1972-1974	Bonneville
P	1972-1974	Grand Ville
S	1972-1974	Firebird

T	1972-1974	Firebird Esprit
U	1972-1974	Firebird Formula
V	1972-1974	Firebird Trans Am
Y	1972	Ventura II
Y	1973-1974	Ventura
Z	1973-1974	Ventura Custom

Third and fourth numbers (69) designates body type.

17	1973-1974	Ventura Hatchback 2 dr
27	1972-1974	Ventura 2 dr
27	1972	Le Mans 2 dr
29	1973-1974	Le Mans 4 dr Sdn
35	1973-1974	Le Mans and Grand Ville Stn Wgn 2 seat
35	1974	Le Mans Luxury Stn Wgn
35	1972-1974	Catalina Stn Wgn 2 seat
35	1972	Bonneville Stn Wgn 2 seat
36	1972	Le Mans Stn Wgn 2 seat DATG
37	1972	Le Mans 2 dr HT
37	1973-1974	Le Mans Grand Am and Sport Sport Coupe
37	1972-1974	Le Mans Luxury Sport Coupe
39	1972-1974	Catalina and Bonneville Sport 4 dr Sdn
39	1972	Le Mans Luxury, Catalina Brougham, and Bonneville 4 dr Sdn
40	1972	Bonneville Special SWB Chassis
45	1972-1974	Catalina and Grand Ville Stn Wgn 3 seat
45	1972	Bonneville Stn Wgn 3 seat
46	1972	Le Mans Stn Wgn 3 seat
47	1972-1974	Grand Ville Sport Coupe
49	1972-1974	Grand Ville Sport 4 dr Sdn
57	1972-1974	Catalina and Bonneville Sport Coupe
57	1972	Catalina Brougham Sport Coupe
67	1972-1974	Grand Ville Convert
67	1972	Catalina Convert
69	1972-1974	Ventura, Catalina, and Bonneville 4 dr Sdn
69	1972	Catalina Brougham 4 dr Sdn
87	1972-1974	Firebird (include Tran Am, Formula 400, and Esprit) 2 dr HT
90	1973-1974	Grand Ville Special LWB Chassis
90	1972	Bonneville Special LWB Chassis

Fifth letter (A) designates engine.

A	1974	350CI	V8	4 Brl Carb
B	1974	350CI	V8	4 Brl Carb
D	1972-1974	250CI	6 Cyl	1 Brl Carb
F	1972-1973	307CI	V8	2 Brl Carb
M	1972-1974	350CI	V8	2 Brl Carb
N	1972-1974	350CI	V8	4 Brl Carb
P	1972-1974	400CI	V8	4 Brl Carb
R	1972-1974	400CI	V8	2 Brl Carb
S	1972-1974	400CI	V8	4 Brl Carb
T	1972-1974	400CI	V8	2 Brl Carb
U	1972	455CI	V8	2 Brl Carb
V	1972	455CI	V8	2 Brl Carb
W	1972-1974	455CI	V8	4 Brl Carb
X	1972-1974	455CI	V8	4 Brl Carb
Y	1972-1974	455CI	V8	4 Brl Carb

Sixth number (4) designates year model.

2	1972
3	1973
4	1974

Seventh letter (A) designates assembly plant.

A	1972-1974	Atlanta, Ga.
C	1972-1974	South Gate, Calif.
D	1972-1973	Doraville, Ga.
G	1972-1974	Framingham, Mass.
L	1972-1974	Van Nuys, Calif.
N	1972-1974	Norwood, Ohio
P	1972-1974	Pontiac, Mich.
W	1972 and 1974	Willow Run, Mich.
X	1972-1974	Kansas City, Kan.
Z	1972-1974	Fremont, Calif.
1	1972-1974	Oshawa, Ontario, Canada
2	1972	St. Therese, Canada

The last six numbers are the sequential production numbers.
V.I.N. plates for most imported 1971 to 1974 foreign cars are located same location as were the 1970 models.

VOLKSWAGEN

1971 to 1974. (supplements information found on page 193)

1971 to 1973.

V.I.N. plates are located left side of dash visible through windshield.
1974.

V.I.N. plates are located left side of dash visible through windshield except:

BEETLE: top center of dash visible through windshield.

DASHER:left windshield post about 4 inches above dash visible through windshield.

THING: top of front hood lock brace right of center. Front hood must be opened.

Sample V.I.N. number:

1341234567

1970 to 1974

118123456

1965 to 1969

First two numbers (13) designates the body series. The third number (4) designates year model. The last seven numbers are the sequential production numbers for 1970 to 1974; six sequential numbers for 1965 to 1969.

Series	Description	
13	Super Beetle	
18	Thing	
32	Dasher	
41-42	412	Sedans
46	412	Stn Wgns

Year Designates

1	1971
2	1972
3	1973
4	1974